AFRICANS AND AMERICANS

AFRICANS AND AMERICANS
Embracing Cultural Differences

Joseph L. Mbele

Africonexion
Northfield, Minnesota, USA

Contents

Acknowledgements

I am grateful to the United States, for a Fulbright grant which enabled me to study at the University of Wisconsin- Madison, 1980-86. I wish to thank Earthwatch and the Center for Field Research. I am grateful to the Americans and Africans with whom I discussed life in Africa and America. I presented some of my ideas to groups of American students at the University of Dar es Salaam and at St. Olaf College, as well as at the African Studies Conference at Colorado College, September 24-26, 2004, which was sponsored by the Associated Colleges of the Midwest, Knox College and Colorado College. I wish to thank the organizers of those events and the audiences. Thanks to Liz Spencer, Whitney Kidd and Jennifer Johnson. Thanks to my immediate family--Heribertha, Deta, Assumpta, and Zawadi--for putting up with my endless travels and flights of fancy. My special gratitude goes to John and Robin Greenler, professors at Beloit College, for urging me to write this booklet and for their unwavering support. For the views in this booklet, however, I alone am accountable.

Introduction

This booklet deals with differences between African and American culture. I noted these differences during my graduate studies at the University of Wisconsin-Madison, 1980-86. I used to spend much time with fellow African students joking about American ways. We wondered why, for example, the police often arrived at parties, to report complaints by neighbours that the music was too loud. What was the purpose of a party, we wondered, if not to have a good time, and how could anyone have a good time if the music was not loud? Compared to African parties, American parties seemed like funerals.

I started thinking about these differences after coming to St. Olaf College, Minnesota, in 1991, to introduce courses in Post-colonial and Third World Literatures. Discussing poetry, drama, and fiction from around the world, my students and I explored different cultures. Over the years, I have also been advising study abroad programs run by U.S colleges and universities in partnership with African universities. I have participated in planning, developing, implementing and evaluating these programs, as well as advising American students on African social and cultural issues, both before and after their stay in Africa. Several times, I have accompanied these students to Tanzania, giving them orientation on Tanzanian social, political and cultural life.

I have also talked with Africans about life in America. Some of them were planning to come to America, and others were just interested in hearing about it. I have enjoyed talking with my fellow Tanzanians, noting how perplexed and intrigued they are by the differences between American and

African ways. I strive to help the Africans coming to America to understand and deal with the cultural challenges I know so well. I know that cultural differences can cause misunderstandings. I tell the Africans, for example, that Americans are so busy with their own work that they scarcely have time to be with visitors or with one another. It is difficult for the Africans to grasp this, until they experience life in America. Sooner or later they begin to feel lonely or neglected.

These conversations have helped me identify topics for this booklet. I do not know any book that deals with these issues in a simple, memorable way. Orientation for study abroad programs tends to be sketchy, with snippets of information about many things, and readings on the history, economic, political, and social conditions of the country to be visited. I wonder how helpful those materials are, and whether students actually read them. I wanted a book that would be more down to earth and practical, one that would teach an American how to venture into a crowded African market, buy a live chicken, and then fend off the throng of hawkers trying to sell him more live chickens, shoes and coconuts. I wanted a book that would attempt to reveal the soul and spirit of human beings: Africans and Americans, in this case. Though this booklet doesn't meet this goal, I hope it provides some helpful insights.

In writing this booklet, I thought about being neutral and objective, but wondered whether that is possible or desirable. I bear in mind Ina Corinne Brown's observation:

> People in different cultures are
> pleased, concerned, annoyed, or
> embarrassed about different things because

they perceive situations in terms of different sets of premises. We are so accustomed to the conventions of our own perceptual world that we lose sight of the fact that such conventions are learned, and that without them our perceptions would not be the same. An American who showed an African village woman a picture postcard of the Empire State Building was startled when the woman exclaimed: "What a beautiful garden!" Not until then did the American become conscious of the basis of his own perception of the picture as that of a tall building.[1]

We tend to value objectivity and scorn subjectivity. Do we really know why? Since I am presenting my experiences and sentiments, which are personal and subjective, I want only to be truthful. I embrace my ideas, emotions, and contradictions, sharing them with you.

Discussing Africans and Americans, I am simplifying a complex topic. There are many cultures in Africa; what I say might apply more to rural than urban areas. Africa, especially urban Africa, bears influences of European and other foreign cultures. America is not homogeneous either. There are Californians and New Yorkers, Texans and Kentuckians, city dwellers and farmers. Some Americans have deep roots in their country, going back hundreds of years; others are recent immigrants from different parts of the world, including Africa. Above all, there are the Native Americans, whose culture goes back thousands of years. Is the idea of Africans and Americans a kind

---

[1] Ina Corinne Brown, *Understanding Other Cultures* (Englewood Cliffs: Prentice-Hall, Inc. 1963), 78-79.

of fiction? I don't know. Sometimes I use the term Africans to mean only black Africans, and I use the term America to mean the USA. In both Africa and the USA, there are many people who resist the culture they live in and struggle to create alternatives. I do not talk about these people here. Overall, I may be guilty of generalizing, but, bearing in mind my overall intentions, I derive comfort from Shakespeare's statement, "To do a great right, do a little wrong."[2]

I am fascinated by folklore and literature; they are the gateways to the soul of a people. Folklore, in particular, is a most reliable index of a people's thoughts and feelings, being the distillation of their collective experience across the ages. Accordingly, I invoke folklore and literature again and again. I learned a great deal from studying folktales, as I demonstrate in my *Matengo Folktales*,[3] and I always try to immerse myself in the folklore of the people I interact with.

Finally, this booklet is not a scholarly study; it is more like a collection of a traveler's tales, anecdotes and thoughts. I wanted it to be that way, making me feel that I am talking to fellow human beings. I hope it will generate discussion, more tales, anecdotes, and thoughts.

---

[2] William Shakespeare, *The Merchant of Venice*, IV, i. ed. W. Moelwyn Merchant (London: Penguin Books, 1987).
[3] Joseph L. Mbele, *Matengo Folktales* (Haverford: Infinity Publishing.com, 2001).

Being a Stranger

This booklet is about crossing cultural boundaries, stepping outside our comfort zone. As soon as we enter a foreign culture, we feel more or less out of place. I felt this way when I went to teach my first class at St. Olaf College, in early September 1991. I had just arrived from Tanzania. I will never forget how tense I was that day, sandwiched among a crowd of white students, fresh from high school. They must have been ill at ease as well, sitting in that classroom with a strange-looking professor, who spoke with a foreign accent. I never thought about their plight, however, being totally caught up in my own uneasiness.

Many people experience such situations, although not always in a bad way. Colleen McElroy, an African-American, narrates her experiences in Madagascar:

> More than once while I was in Madagascar, I found myself measuring the thin line between family and stranger, especially when I was mistaken for Malagasy, my facial features reminding someone of a Betsileo or Bara friend, or a Sakalava neighbor. Of course, I only needed to attempt a few words in Malagasy, laminated by my midwestern accent, for anyone to recognize that I was a *vahiny*, a stranger. But nevertheless, I was asked, sometimes simply because I resembled a friend who had recently immigrated to the West, or the child or perhaps the grandchild of that person. And always, even when I was asked how far I had

traveled and how long would I stay, I was an outsider made to feel welcome.[4]

East Africans call a white person mzungu, and in parts of West Africa, they use the word toubab, as we see, for example, in Sembene Ousmane's novel, *God's Bits of Wood*.[5] In the African villages, the sight of a mzungu causes much excitement. Some people will stare at a mzungu, out of curiosity or wonderment. The children will follow a mzungu around, curious and amused. The smaller children and babies might scream in terror. Gradually, however, what was strange begins to appear normal. In Africa, the little children do get used to the mzungu and come into his or her house to talk and play. I have undergone the same change. These days, I sit with a crowd of white people without being overly aware, let alone caring, that I am different.

While such developments take place, certain problems remain; for example, the Africans who have never been abroad believe all white people are wealthy. These Africans have never seen a poor white person and don't believe there is any such person. In addition, they consider every mzungu intelligent and reliable; they trust a mzungu more than they do fellow Africans. This is largely a legacy of colonialism, as Fanon pointed out.[6]

---

[4] Colleen J. McElroy, *Over the Lip of the World: Among the Storytellers of Madagascar* (Seattle: University of Washington Press, 1999), 157-8.

[5] Sembene Ousmane, *Gods Bits of Wood*, trans. Francis Price (London: Heinemann, 1970).

[6] Frantz Fanon, *The Wretched of the Earth*, trans. Constance Farrington (New York: Grove Press, 1963) and *Black Skin White Masks*, trans. Charles Lam Markmann (New York: Grove Wiedenfeld, 1991).

Africans might call a fellow black African mzungu. This can be a positive or a negative attribute, depending on the situation. An African who is always punctual, especially as a matter of choice, earns the name mzungu, not an entirely bad attribute, just a little odd. An African in authority who pushes subordinates to be always punctual will be called mzungu, an indication of both scorn and resentment. An African who puts on airs, behaving, dressing, or talking like a white person, is called mzungu. In this context, the term is almost always sarcastic or scornful. In many parts of Africa, African-Americans find themselves in an awkward situation, because they are black and speak only English. The Africans initially assume they are just fellow Africans who are putting on airs. Even after learning that this black person is from America, they might still call him or her mzungu, without the negative connotation. It is virtually impossible for the African-Americans to assume native African characteristics. If they learn the local language, for example, they speak it like white people. We all face this issue of mother tongue interference when we speak a foreign language.

Of course, African-Americans don't expect to be called white people. The Africans mean no offense; they just don't understand American racial politics. Having grown up in Africa, they don't share the racial consciousness and feelings of the Americans. It is easy, therefore, for Africans and African-Americans to misunderstand one another. Certain concepts that African-Americans take for granted are unknown to the Africans. For example, Africans don't see or define themselves as people of colour, a phrase that Americans of all races use. Some Africans call African-Americans niggers, believing that it is a normal and acceptable term.

Race is a major issue in America. Hardly a day goes by without some news, discussion, or problem connected with race. Race-consciousness pervades the lives of the Americans. Whenever a white and a non-white American meet or interact, the racial factor creeps in. The white person comes under surveillance and has to be wary of saying anything that can be considered racist. Due to the history of slavery, the situation is worse if it involves a white American and an African-American. Coming from such a background, white Americans might assume that Africans are like African-Americans. They might strive to be careful in dealing with Africans, the way they do with African-Americans. The truth is that Africans are not African-Americans, just as African-Americans are not Africans, at least from a cultural perspective.

The experience of blacks and whites in Africa is different from what it is in the USA. Africans see white people in a different way from the way African-Americans see them. The typical African might know only a few white people, usually missionaries, doctors, or teachers, who are kindly, benevolent and respected figures. Only in a few places, such as South Africa under apartheid, have Africans experienced the kind of racial dynamics that African-Americans and other non-white Americans know so well. Africans in Africa are not alienated and powerless in the way African-Americans are in America. They have a strong sense of self, and pride in their identity, even if they might appear humble.

Africans come to America with this mindset. Not programmed to watch out for racism all the time, not conditioned to see, hear, or feel the presence of racism the way African-Americans do, Africans are generally comfortable interacting with

8

white people, including those that African-Americans might consider difficult to deal with. Unlike African-Americans, Africans are not burdened with a legacy of slavery, with its numerous psychological, social, and other effects. These differences often cause misunderstandings between Africans and African-Americans. The African-Americans see Africans as naïve and ignorant about racism, and the Africans wonder why the African-Americans have such negative attitudes towards white people. This problem has other dimensions. The Africans start with the belief that African-Americans are their brothers and sisters. Sooner or later, the truth sets in, that Africans and African-Americans belong to two different cultures. Americans of all races share certain values and perspectives, including particular sensitivities to race issues. Africans don't know, for example, that in American culture, blue eyes and blonde hair signify beauty. To Africans, the very idea of blue eyes is somewhat frightening.

Returning from Africa, white American students note that the experience of being a minority there changed their perspective on life. A few complain that some Africans stared at them. I tell them that, here in the USA, some Americans stare at me too. Such experiences make us uncomfortable, but they are useful. By being with them, we give the other people the opportunity to meet someone different from them. We ourselves taste what strangers in our midst might be experiencing. We can, thereby, develop empathy with them. Without such opportunities, we might remain trapped in ignorance and prejudice. After several years of giving orientation to American students going to Africa, I decided to change the way I talked about experiencing a foreign culture.

Bearing in mind that there are foreign students in American colleges, I began asking the American students whether they interacted with the foreign students. Now, I always urge them to do so. To experience or learn about a foreign culture, we do not need to wait until we travel to foreign countries.

Being in a foreign culture, we sometimes wish that culture would adjust itself to accommodate us. In America, non-white students in predominantly white colleges often express such sentiments. They complain about the lack of a welcoming environment. I have mixed feelings about this. I value the challenge of living in a foreign culture as an opportunity to learn about that culture and about myself. For a non-white person, a predominantly white college is such a foreign culture. As long as the institution treats every person with fairness and justice, I don't think it should change its character and traditions simply because of the presence of a minority group. I cannot imagine, for example, an African university changing itself on account of the presence of a few Americans. I am not sure, either, that a predominantly black university in America would think about changing its character because of the presence of a few white students. We go to college to be challenged, to broaden and enrich our experiences and perspectives.

This, however, is not a problem of non-white students alone. It is a general American problem. Across the USA, one hears complaints from students about professors from abroad, who speak English in ways Americans find difficult to follow. Instead of viewing this as an opportunity to broaden their abilities, the Americans demand that the foreigners speak like Americans. I always tell my American students that this attitude is not healthy. In African schools and colleges, one finds teachers from different parts of the world, including Americans. The Africans don't demand that the foreigners speak English like Africans; they just learn to understand them. I believe it is in the best interest of the Americans to make their ears equally versatile.

Interestingly, many white American students go to Africa to experience a different culture and its challenges. They say this in their application forms for study abroad. For them, Africa is culturally the ultimate foreign place. We can learn from these students; they don't ask the African institutions to Americanize themselves. In fact, in their quest for the most challenging situations, these students choose to live with African families. They greatly appreciate these home stays as the most authentic cultural experiences. On the other hand, African-American students may want to go to Africa believing they will feel at home, because Africa is the Motherland. Such expectations easily turn into disappointments, as Africa poses unique cultural challenges to the African-Americans. Ama Ata Aidoo's play *Dilemma of a Ghost* explores this theme very well.[7] It depicts an African-American woman who meets a young Ghanaian in the USA and marries him. She is excited by the prospect of going to Africa, the Motherland. She goes there with him, finally, only to encounter frustration and misery due to cultural differences.

Americans who have been to Africa note that Africans are friendly. Hemingway recorded his experiences with the Maasai:

---

[7] Ama Ata Aidoo, *The Dilemma of a Ghost and Anowa* (London: Longman African Writers, 1995).

Seeing them running and so damned handsome and so happy made us all happy. I had never seen such quick disinterested friendliness, nor such fine looking people.... They had that attitude that makes brothers, that unexpressed but instant and complete acceptance that you must be Masai wherever it is you come from. That attitude you only get from the best of the English, the best of the Hungarians and the very best Spaniards; the thing that used to be the most clear distinction of nobility when there was nobility. It is an ignorant attitude and the people who have it do not survive, but very few pleasanter things ever happen to you than the encountering of it.[8]

Whenever Americans told me about the friendliness of the Africans, I used to wonder why they did that, asking myself whether such friendliness was absent or unusual in American society. Gradually, I realized that Americans don't warm up to strangers until after being introduced. They teach their children not to talk to strangers. I read an article, written by an American, about the behaviour of American students abroad, with some advice about avoiding risky behaviour, such as asking strangers for help or directions. This amazed me; in Africa, asking strangers for directions is not risky behaviour. Often, the strangers will not only give you directions, but will escort you some distance, or even walk with you to your destination. Parents will ask their children to escort a stranger. It is a normal task for African children. One evening, I

---

[8] Ernest Hemingway, *Green Hills of Africa* (New York: Simon and Schuster, 1996), 221.

was on the outskirts of Dar es Salaam, on my way to deliver a message to the relatives of a Tanzanian living in the USA. After walking through banana groves and gardens, I stopped at a house, greeted the woman who was there, and asked for directions. It was getting dark. She called out her little daughter and told her to escort me to the place I was looking for. As we walked, I kept telling myself that this would never happen in the USA. After she showed me the house, she went back home. This is an example of what the Africans mean when they say that it takes a village to raise a child. That mother sent her child on this errand and knew that I would take care of her.

I recall a different episode, which happened in Northfield, Minnesota. I was driving up a street while it was raining. Ahead of me, on the sidewalk, a young girl was walking in the same direction I was going, without an umbrella. I knew that in Tanzania, I could have stopped my car and given her a ride. But this was the USA, and I was afraid that if I stopped my car, she might be alarmed. I was a complete stranger, and a black man at that. With considerable sadness, I kept driving and passed her.

I have often told my American students that in Tanzania, children coming from school stand on the roadside and hitch hike rides home from anybody who drives by, whether known to them or complete strangers. These people pick up the children and drive on, stopping to let out any child who says he or she has arrived home.

Health and Safety

The thought of going abroad brings excitement to Africans but anxieties to Americans. While Africans assume that things will be fine, Americans worry about safety, seeing the world outside America as dangerous and the body as vulnerable and fragile. Before a trip abroad, Americans go to great lengths to fortify themselves against infections and other hazards they believe await them out there. They consult doctors, to ensure that their bodies are in good condition, the way we consult a mechanic before a long trip, to see that our old car works well. They consult the Center for Disease Control in Atlanta and State Department travel advisories for the latest information about the health and safety conditions in the area they are traveling to. They take trip-related medications and inoculations very seriously. Africans will take such inoculations if pressured, but they consider them a mere inconvenience. Give an African the chance to go abroad, a ticket and money, and he or she will head straight to the airport. Africans take it for granted that the human body works well. They do not even think about it. They know that what is destined to happen will happen. "Ajali haina kinga," states a Swahili proverb: there is no antidote against misfortune.

To appreciate that Africans have a different attitude to safety, just observe their transportation system: trains, trucks, buses, minibuses and other vehicles speed along, crowded with people, with some hanging from the doors and windows or perched on the roof. African drivers see driving as a heroic adventure; their goal is speeding, overtaking, and preventing anyone from overtaking them. In his play, *The Road,* Soyinka touches on this theme.[9] Peter Chilson's *Riding the Demon* presents an engaging account of the African roads and the driving culture.[10] When I was growing up, we had a song urging drivers to speed:

Dereva, chechema,
Chechema na mwendo.
Dereva, chechema,
Chechema na mwendo,
Tupate kuona ufundi wa kwako,
Tupate kuona ufundi wa kwako.

Driver, strive harder,
Strive harder and speed up.
Driver, strive harder,
Strive harder and speed up,
So we can see your driving skill,
So we can see your driving skill.

Over the years, I have participated in many official and informal discussions with Americans about safety for Americans abroad: what Americans should do or not do, what hazards lurk out there, what medications to take or not take, what to do in case of emergencies, and plans for the evacuation of Americans, if necessary. In official meetings, these discussions seemed endless, tormenting my spirit. The longer they lasted, the more I suffered. For comic relief, I let my mind dwell on Shakespeare's words: "Cowards die many times before their deaths."[11] The more the Americans

---

[9] Wole Soyinka, *The Road* (London: Oxford University Press, 1965).
[10] Peter Chilson, *Riding the Demon: On the Road in West Africa* (Athens: University of Georgia Press, 1999).
[11] William Shakespeare, *Julius Caesar*, II, ii. ed. David Bevington (Toronto: Bantam Classics, 1988.

talked about the hazards in other countries, especially African countries, the more they seemed to imply that the United States was a very safe place, perhaps the safest in the world. I saw these conversations not really as occasions for sharing useful information but as reinforcements of American propaganda.

The briefings Americans get before going abroad are not even-handed; stressing how Americans should protect themselves while abroad, these briefings tend to imply that only the Americans are in danger. For example, while admonishing Americans to take precautions against sexually transmitted diseases, these briefings do not even suggest that Americans could infect the other people. They present, in effect, a fantasy of Americans as disease-free.

Even when they are not traveling abroad, Americans tend to focus on health and safety in ways that other people will find excessive. They worry a great deal about illnesses. I have read reports that at least forty percent of the Americans are on medication of some sort. Whenever American doctors give a prescription, they ask not only whether you have allergies, but also whether you are on medication. Since I was routinely not on medication, I felt, while talking to the doctor, as if I was violating some cultural norm. I always wonder whether all the medications that Americans take are for real or imagined illnesses, but one thing is clear: drug companies promote this situation and make money out of it.

Keith Richburg, an African-American, exemplifies the American behaviour quite well. He writes:

Before I first set out for Africa, I went to the traveler's clinic at Georgetown University Hospital in Washington and subjected myself to a dizzying array of injections for almost every conceivable ailment—hepatitis, tetanus, typhoid, even rabies. I was told there were a lot of stray dogs roaming the streets, and having some of the initial rabies shots in Washington before I left might save me the series of painful shots in the stomach later on if I were unfortunate enough to cross the path of a stray canine.[12]

Richburg took many measures to protect himself, including a yearlong supply of malaria tablets.[13] He continues:

Daily living in Africa is also a constant battle to ward off possible disease and infection from the water you drink, cook with, and bathe in....Even something as simple as brushing your teeth—an act that an American takes for granted every day—can result in a nasty bout of diarrhea or worse....On those trips, I always made sure to carry an adequate supply of bottled water--sometimes a boxful, if I suspected I might be on the road for a long haul. To brush my teeth, I'd first dip the bristles into the water, apply the toothpaste, and then rinse my mouth and the toothbrush with the bottled water. I was always mindful not to waste too much, since

---

[12] Keith B. Richburg, *Out of America: A Black Man Confronts Africa* (New York: Basic Books, 1997), 129.
[13] Richburg, 129.

bottled water was a precious and often costly commodity.[14]

As time went, Richburg began to see the absurdity of his fears. He took his malaria pills "religiously for the first few months, but then dropped the routine. It was better to take my chances with mosquito netting and repellent, I learned, than stick to that regimen over three years and perhaps only lower my resistance."[15] He also says:

> Even while taking precautions, though, I knew it was impossible to wrap myself in a protective bubble. I often ended up just plunging in and taking a chance—like sitting down for tea with Somali elders in Baidoa town, not knowing how they managed to wash the little teacups, or sharing my water bottle with a Rwandan Tutsi soldier in Byumba because it was the polite thing to do."[16]

From an African perspective, Richburg's comment about the elders is offensive, but I will leave it aside, only pointing out the irony in his subsequent admission: "I was never seriously sick in Africa, despite all the sickness and disease around me every day. But serious, I suppose, depends on one's definition; diarrhea and occasional stomach pains were kind of constant."[17] Despite his paranoia, Richburg admits: "And yet in Africa, people would walk around for weeks, years,

---

[14] Richburg, 130.
[15] Richburg, 130.
[16] Richburg, 130-1.
[17] Richburg, 131.

a lifetime, without ever setting foot in a hospital."[18] He does not, however, fully understand why the Africans don't seem to need hospital visits as badly as Americans do. He thinks it is because of the expense or, as in the case of Somalia, the danger of traveling to the hospitals, but he does not understand an even more basic reason: the Africans do not worry about diseases and safety the way Americans do.

Americans worry about getting ill because health care and medicine are very expensive in America. However, I don't think this is the only reason. It is clear to me that Americans dread illness much more than other people do. Even rich Americans, who could easily afford any medical expenses, worry excessively about health and illness. Another reason is that America is a land of lawsuits; everybody seems to be waiting to sue someone. Colleges, travel companies, and other institutions sending Americans abroad take extraordinary measures to ensure their own safety from lawsuits. I have observed first hand the kind of precautions American colleges and universities take. In the event of any trouble or potential trouble in the foreign location, they take drastic measures, such as canceling a program or evacuating students back to America, presumably the land of safety.

How safe is America? When they are at home, in America, Americans worry about safety on their streets and in their neighbourhoods. In the cities, most Americans would think twice before venturing into poor neighbourhoods. Those who can afford it, move out of the inner cities to the suburbs, because the inner cities are not safe. Adults escort school children to the bus stops. Even the

---

[18] Richburg, 131.

playgrounds are unsafe, and adults watch the children at play. However, when they think about going abroad, the Americans forget all this and think only of the dangers in the other countries. If the destination is Africa, the worries multiply, for Africa is the place the Americans consider a kind of hell on earth, plagued by wars, diseases and pestilence. The American media overflows with such images, and demonizing Africa seems to help Americans feel good about their own country. The Africans themselves, however, see and experience their continent in quite a different way. Americans who visit Africa see that Africans are a cheerful people. That is what struck me the most, on my first day in America. I did not see the kind of bright and cheerful faces I used to see in Tanzania.

Once in the foreign country, Americans closely monitor what they eat and drink, where they step, sleep, and so on. They particularly fear the water: not just the drinking water, but the bathing water and the water for brushing teeth. At the slightest sign of trouble in the body, the Americans rush to a doctor, to find out what is wrong. Should a mosquito venture into their bedroom, they panic, believing, perhaps, it will kill them. Not long ago, the American media reported that some species of mosquito was flying from the southern states northwards. I was amused that a mere mosquito got such attention. One consequence of all this is that, when Americans are abroad, especially in third world countries, they tend to be demanding on their hosts, regarding safety issues. The Africans need to understand this; otherwise, they will be puzzled to see Americans worrying a great deal about what the Africans consider trivial matters, such as a cough or a running nose. Worse still, they might resent the Americans for the trouble they will cause when so afflicted. It is equally important for Americans to understand the African attitudes. Otherwise, they will think that the Africans don't care about them.

There is a humourous side to the issue, however. Americans visiting Africa or any third world country worry a great deal about eating a banana or a mango being sold in the market. However, if that mango makes it to a grocery store in America, the Americans readily buy and eat it. Miracles still happen.

It appears that Americans and Africans respond to crises somewhat differently. When something bad happens to Americans abroad, such as a stomach upset or a mosquito bite, they make a big issue of out it. Should they lose a purse, they send the news back to the USA. In 1989, my suitcase was stolen in Atlanta, but I never told anyone in Tanzania. I know such things could happen anywhere in the world. I think, as I have suggested, Americans go out of their country fearing the worst, and when a problem happens, it comes as a self-fulfilling prophecy. Relaying the news back to the USA reinforces the myths that America has about itself and about other countries.

We can observe these cultural differences in other situations, such as the hospitals. A hospital visit in Africa is a different experience from such a visit in America. In America, doctors spend much time listening to a patient. They explore all kinds of issues regarding the patient's problem, even those that might seem peripheral, before prescribing treatment. They will talk about the medicine, when and under what conditions it should be taken, and its possible side effects. They will ask the patient whether he or she has allergies to any medication or is currently on medication. Sometimes, before administering any injection or medication, the doctors will ask the patients or their guardians to sign a consent form. Sometimes, they will say they need to consult some other specialist.

I once discussed the issue of American doctors with a Somali social worker in Minnesota. She said that when Somali patients hear an American doctor saying he or she will consult other doctors, they wonder why. A doctor is supposed to know everything; if he must consult others, he is certainly not good enough. In Africa, a doctor has the authority to diagnose ailments, prescribe cures, and enforce them. American doctors sometimes seek the patient's consent before administering medication or other treatment. Africans will find this idea very strange. In most cases, patients do not even know the names of the medicines. Americans, because of their extraordinary concern with health issues, tend to know a great deal. They read and listen to different experts all the time. No wonder they have such long conversations with doctors.

As I have mentioned, however, Africans trust the body more than Americans do, and are confident that the body handles medication well. Such a positive attitude, as experts say, does help people stay healthy or respond well to medication. If they take medicine and experience adverse side effects, the Africans merely go back to the doctor for treatment. They do not complain and would never sue a doctor for such a problem. This attitude stems from the age-old tradition of dealing with healers: people took their sick to the healer and let the healer do his work. They trusted and respected the healer. That is their attitude to doctors even today. I have heard American doctors talking about the respect and trust they experienced while working in African hospitals.

Visiting a sick person in the hospital, Americans take flowers and cards. Africans take things the patient can eat or use: cooked food, fruits, soft drinks, or money. A gift of flowers or cards will baffle the typical African patient. Barley tells us more about the African ways:

> When a man is ill, his whole family insist on being there, cooking there, doing the washing, nursing the children and conducting domestic affairs in strident voices as if at home. There are blaring radios, hawkers peddling a hundred forms of trash, long queues of swaddled women and downcast men all clutching pieces of paper like charms.[19]

Barley observes the situation with an outsider's eyes and ought to pay some attention to the local perspective. The Africans see the health and well being of the individual as intertwined with the health and well being of the community. This drives the Africans to stay together. African beliefs about health and illness often involve the influence of supernatural forces, which have to be countered with charms and other magic means. The hospital, like the healer's compound, is charged with forces, seen and unseen, which aid or hinder the patient's recovery. One can understand why the people Barley describes would treat a doctor's prescriptions like charms.

[19] Nigel Barley, *Adventures in a Mud Hut: An Innocent Anthropologist Abroad* (New York: The Vanguard Press, 1983), 115.

Food, Drink, and Hospitality

Every African culture has its own concepts, customs, beliefs, attitudes and taboos regarding food. Unlike Americans, Africans tend to have a rigid concept of what is food or proper food and what is not food or proper food. Rice eaters stick to rice, the same goes for bananas eaters, ugali eaters and so on. There are subtle rules and customs concerning food. Certain portions of an animal or a chicken are for men only. In my own Matengo culture, the gizzard of a chicken is for men. In some cultures, expectant women are not allowed to eat certain foods. When hunters kill an animal, they divide it in a certain way among themselves or the people in the village. Americans think a great deal about the nutritional aspects of food: calories, carbohydrates, vitamins, proteins, fibers and such things. In this way, it seems to me, the idea of food as food is disappearing from the American consciousness. Africans still know and eat food, with down-to-earth names like fufu, ugali and matoke.

When I was studying in Madison, I told some American friends that we Africans eat the same kind of food every day, all our lives. One of them wondered whether we don't get bored. That surprised me; the idea that the food we eat would be boring never occurs to us. We differ from Americans, who look for variety and choice. At the same time, people in my village pity me, when I tell them what we eat in America. When I take American students to Tanzania, I look for ways to explain this to them. I told one group that, just as there is the American Dream, there is the Tanzanian Dream, and the Tanzanian Dream includes having the same kind of food every day, such as ugali, rice, or bananas. When they found themselves in that situation, they joked about living the Tanzanian Dream. This helped keep their spirits high throughout their stay.

Americans tend to have fixed meal times. When the time for lunch or dinner comes, parents summon children home to eat. Africans eat when they are hungry, not when a clock indicates it is time to eat. African children will be out playing and will only come home when they are hungry. In America, guests declare in advance whether they will come for lunch or dinner. In Africa, guests just arrive, and the hosts cook for them, even at night, without asking them if they need food. Asking implies one is not hospitable. Americans ask, with good intentions.

In Africa, eating is a ritual. It starts with the washing of hands, the oldest person washing first, followed by the next oldest, down to the youngest. Africans wash hands before eating, even if cutlery is provided, and even in restaurants. This is not the case in America. People sit at the dinner table and soon start eating, without washing their hands. I remember the day I took my two young daughters to a restaurant in the USA, soon after their arrival from Tanzania. After the waiter had set the food on our table, my daughters dashed to the women's room to wash their hands, while I just sat there, ready to eat.

In Africa, food has much social and symbolic meaning. When people are eating, they will invite you to join them. You have to, even if you have just eaten somewhere else. It is improper to refuse food. Eating with other people affirms togetherness and the goodness of your spirit. Africans believe that eating alone is not good for one's health. In traditional Matengo society, the women used to put the food at a communal place called sengu, where everybody could eat it. A husband has to eat the food his wife cooks. Refusing to do so implies that he has another woman somewhere who is taking care of him. In many languages, the word for eating is the same as the word for having sex; the concept of feeding covers both offering food and offering sex. Coming from such a culture, I find the American concept of fast food a kind of taboo violation.

Many Americans like to invite foreigners home for dinner. This happens any time during the year, but especially on Thanksgiving Day. Often, there will be a number of guests. In the invitation, the hosts specify the time the dinner will be served, and it is served on time. It is very important for Africans to remember this. There will be plenty of food, and different kinds of drinks. There will be things, though, that will surprise the Africans. One of these is the appetizer, an alien concept to Africans. Then, as the dinner comes to an end, the hosts offer the guests coffee or dessert, which can be some type of ice cream. African meals do not have desserts. The fact that at the end of the meal, Americans will take coffee, after drinking something else, such as beer or wine, has always struck me as strange. We Africans tend to be consistent: if we start with beer, we stick with it. When the Americans switch to coffee, we would rather have another beer, unless there is none left.

Often, the Americans will host receptions. There are likely to be many people there, crowding about the house. I had difficulties when I first attended these receptions. The hosts warmly welcomed me, as they welcomed everybody, and cheerfully urged me to feel at home, and to help myself to the food and the drinks. When Americans say this, they mean it: you should feel free to take whatever food and drink you need and even go and get them from the fridge. I had just come from Africa, where the idea of a guest going into the host's fridge is unacceptable, unless the guest is a relative of the hosts. Therefore, when the Americans told me to feel at home and help myself, I just sat glued to the couch or chair, even though everybody else was moving about, getting what they wanted, even from the fridge. Fortunately, American hosts are attentive to their guests, and they always spotted me and helped me. As time passed, I became brave enough to go open people's fridges. Nowadays, I am so used to this culture that I can sail through the house like the Americans, greeting people on the way, and heading in the direction of the drinks.

Although they have fixed meal times, Americans also like snacks, which they carry in their cars, to the office, to class, and meetings. They eat the snacks as they drive, walk, or read, even while attending a talk. Africans are quite reserved: they eat only in specific places, such as the home or the restaurant.

Like food, drink is vital in all cultures. What we drink, why, when, where, and how tends to differ from culture to culture. Americans drink a lot of coffee. I come from a coffee growing region, and we have much coffee, but we do not drink it as much as Americans do. Americans drink coffee in all kinds of situations. I found it strange, during my early days in Madison, that professors and students brought coffee to class. I recall that, long before I came to America, during my undergraduate days at the University of Dar es Salaam, there was an old American professor there, who used to bring his thermos flask to class and would drink his coffee during short breaks, in the classroom. For us that was quite a sensation, and we used to talk about it. We did not know that what he was doing was perfectly normal in America.

In Africa, beer is very important; it brings people together, smoothens relationships, and plays a role in various rituals and social situations. A person wishing to win another person's favour or make amends for some wrongdoing offers beer for that purpose. In Kitereza's *Mr. Myombekere*, there are a number of detailed descriptions of beer drinking and the social functions of beer.[20] As Myombekere prepares to go to his in-laws to beg his wife to return to him, he brews beer and takes it to them. Similarly, in *Things Fall Apart*, a needy young man takes beer to an old man from whom he seeks help.[21] I can think of no better and easier way to win hearts in Africa than buying people a beer or two.

The African bar, whether in the village or in the city, is a very important social institution, with its own culture and etiquette. It is a place to meet friends, make friends, cut deals, share information, news, and gossip. In the bar, people tend to be very generous. Everyone with money feels the desire to buy yet another round of beers for everyone at the table. In 1980, while teaching at the university of Burundi, I witnessed an interesting custom. A person would buy a beer and first pour it into the glasses of everyone else at the table, only serving himself last.

When an African invites you out, for a beer or a meal, you know that he or she will pay the bill. You do not need to have money; you just go. If you

---

[20] Aniceti Kitereza, *Mr. Myombekere and his Wife Bugonoka, Their Son Ntulanalwo and Daughter Bulihwali*, trans. Gabriel Ruhumbika (Dar es Salaam: Mkuki na Nyota Publishers, 2002).
[21] Chinua Achebe, *Things Fall Apart* (London: Heinemann, 1981), 14-16.

have money, of course, you buy something as well. In the bar, you can buy roast meat or beer. Roast meat is a great attraction in African bars. In America, things can be complicated, and Africans should watch out. When Americans invite you to a bar or restaurant, you should carry some money, as a precaution. When the eating and drinking is over and the bill comes, Americans tend to split the bill, so that everyone pays his or her share. Although I have lived in America for many years, I always dread this moment. Sometimes, however, the person who invites you will state clearly that he or she will pay the bill. When Americans say this, they mean it. It is enough to just thank them and let them pay.

In East Africa, people use the Swahili word "karibu" again and again. "Karibu" means welcome. People will say "karibu" to you when you are approaching their house, their table in a restaurant or bar, or anywhere they are sitting or standing. People will say "karibu" to acquaintances and complete strangers alike. It is an expression of hospitality. No matter how poor they are, they will welcome you. They don't worry whether they have food in the house, the idea being that even water, or just conversation, is enough. A Swahili proverb says: "Mgeni aje; mwenye nyumba apone," which means, "Let the guest come so that the host may get healing." This proverb expresses a widespread African belief regarding the beneficial effects, in a spiritual sense, at least, of having a guest. During a research visit in a Sukuma village in northwest Tanzania, with my team of Tanzanians, Americans and other foreigners, the villagers welcomed us with a moving song, in which they stated again and again: "Guests heal the homestead."

Hospitality underlies many aspects of African life: an African home may be full of people, but will accept more people. I believe this is the main reason the African buses, minibuses and other vehicles take so many people. When there is unrest in their own countries, Africans easily migrate across the border and settle in the other countries. This has been the case over the ages. Even in normal times, people seemed free to move and settle in other communities. The legends of various ethnic groups routinely narrate the coming of strangers, usually hunters, into a community, where they are welcomed, settle down, and raise families. Today there are laws and international conventions, which require refugees to live in specific areas. These rules conflict with the African traditions, and the ordinary Africans often don't know them or ignore them.

Africans have elaborate customs for treating guests. The host cooks special food for the guest, depending on the status of the guest and also what the host can afford. People strive, however, to provide the best they can. It is quite common for the guest to be left to eat alone. The hosts will not be eating the same food that the guest eats. In *Myombekere*, there are elaborate descriptions of the treatment of guests. In *Matengo Folktales*, I provide some description of the Matengo customs.[22]

In Africa, hospitality and reciprocity go hand in hand. I deal with this cycle all the time. As I do my research in African folklore, I have to find the right way to express my appreciation to the people who help me. This does not always mean giving them money. That could be inappropriate, especially when dealing with elders, who require appropriate

---

[22] Mbele, 91-92.

protocol. If you don't know the appropriate protocol, it is best to seek out and use intermediaries who know the local culture. I often give out money, however, as sign of gratitude. However, when I am dealing with old people, I ask them to accept "a little beer" as I hand them the money. Once the money is defined as "a little beer," it acquires the necessary cultural meaning, which is different from the idea of payment or money.

Conversation

Compared to Americans, Africans talk a great deal. They seize every opportunity to have conversation, even at work. Greetings and introductions in Africa can be elaborate; people want to know not only your name but also something about your family, clan, or the ethnic group; whose son, daughter, sister, brother, wife, or husband you are; where you come from, where you have been, and where you are going. You are not just an individual but part of a community. You are the father, son, brother, husband, or uncle of so and so, or you are the mother, wife, daughter, sister, or aunt of so and so. When, therefore Africans ask how you are doing, they are conscious that your wellbeing is connected to the network of relationships you belong to. Responding to a greeting, such as "how are you today?" an African will surely talk about himself or herself, but will freely talk about family members as well.

Greetings are very important in African culture, and they tend to be elaborate. Ruhumbika describes greetings among the Kerebe as follows:

> The Wakerewe have a very elaborate system of greeting each other for which there is simply no English equivalent. To begin with, they consider greetings so important that a person cannot greet people collectively but has to address an individual salutation to each person in a group of people and if they are too many then to greet as many of them as he or she can. Then the greetings themselves are different, and very much so, depending on whether the two individuals are

peers or a senior and a junior according ranking by age, gender, blood, clan or in-law kinship. Blood and clan kinship ranks always take precedence over age and gender and any other considerations of seniority, so that, for example, a little girl who is a cousin of an old man's mother is his mother's "sister" in their extended family relationship and therefore is greeted by the man with the salutation of respect with which he greets his real mother and other female senior relatives of his, any female cousin of a man's mother-in-law is considered another "mother-in-law" of that man and greeted by him as such irrespective of her age, the paternal aunt of a man's wife is greeted by that man as if she were male and his real father-in-law, a little boy who is a cousin of a man's father is that man's "younger father' and greeted by the man as if he were his real father, and so on. On top of that, all those numerous different salutations are mostly conventional words and phrases with no other independent meaning in the language, so that the English equivalents used here like "Good morning!", "Good evening!" and "How are you" in Kikerewe would be considered not the greetings themselves but follow-ups to greetings or "exchanging news" of each other's welfare.[23]

There is a reason for this, as Afokpa notes:

In Africa, greetings have considerable significance in people's everyday social life.

---

[23] Gabriel Ruhumbika, "Notes," in Kitereza, 14.

Though a daily ritual performance which governs the social interactions between the members of the community as well as strengthening and sealing the relationships between them. For the Eʋe people of South-Togo, greetings essentially constitute "peace-bearing and goodluck speeches," possessing the characteristics of a ritual test as well as the power of an "open sesame" which, when properly performed, bring to the performer all the blessings of which one can dream."[24]

African conversation tends to involve more than merely sharing messages in clear language. It can include mere hints, vague and roundabout statements, especially among elders or in formal occasions. Beating about the bush is often the appropriate way to communicate in Africa. The conversation can, therefore, be slow and prolonged, as the speaker encodes messages in various ways, and the listener tries to determine what the speaker is saying. Achebe's *Things Fall Apart* offers good insights into the nature of African conversation. There is, for example, the occasion when Okoye visits Unoka, to demand payment of a debt:

> Having spoken plainly so far, Okoye said the next half a dozen sentences in proverbs. Among the Ibo the art of conversation is regarded very highly, and proverbs are the palm-oil with which words are eaten. Okoye was a great talker and he spoke for a long time, skirting round the subject and then

---

[24] Kodjo Jb. Afokpa, "Greeting Performance in Eʋeland: Ethnographic Background and Cultural Analysis,' *Southern Folklore*, 48, 3 (1991), 205.

hitting it finally. In short, he was asking Unoka to return the two hundred cowries he had borrowed from him more than two years before.[25]

Africans are particularly mindful of sensitive situations, which require indirection in speech. In such cases, as McElroy notes, "Language, indeed, becomes a means of simultaneously hiding and revealing thought so as to convey delicate and dangerous matters."[26] McElroy is talking about Madagascar, but her observations apply to other parts of Africa. Yankah explains this well:

Indirection may find expression in circumlocution while addressing a sensitive topic, such as loan solicitation (boseabó) or other requests for favors. In such potentially embarrassing situations, the speaker may initially skirt the main subject and divert the attention of his potential benefactor to other issues. In broaching the topic, the speaker may begin from the root of the problem and work his way gradually to the circumstances that led to his need, sometimes confiding delicate but irrelevant domestic information to justify his cause. All this while, he may avoid direct eye contact with his addressee. In his reply, the addressee may adopt a similar strategy and break into a long narration explaining his own situation of need; or he may direct his explanation to a big loan he gave away to another in need, just a moment ago. The use of circumlocution in addressing

[25] Achebe, 5-6.
[26] McElroy, xxix.

sensitive topics appears to be a pervasive phenomenon in West Africa.[27]

Americans wait to be introduced before they are comfortable talking with people they don't know. The introductions are short, usually providing only the first name. The greetings are also short, such as "hi." Africans who live in America are used to this, and they take it in style. However, they do complain about a kind of smile some Americans smile, when they approach from the direction one is going. It is a momentary straining of the lips, without showing the teeth and without any word, such as "hi." This smile does not please the Africans. Africans acknowledge one another and other people by talking.

Americans expect straightforward conversation. Indirection, circumlocution, and lack of eye contact are sure to irritate them, leading them to view the speaker as unreliable or worse. Americans on business trips, for example, want to get to the point right away, get things done according to schedule, so that they can go to the next appointment or task. Unfortunately, this is the surest way to dampen relationships with Africans.

Conversation among young or adult Africans can be very animated, with everyone interrupting everyone else. While Americans consider it inappropriate to interrupt others, Africans don't mind such behaviour; they regard interruptions as a sign of the vitality of the topic being discussed. With many voices raised and competing to be heard, African conversation might seem, to an outsider, like a quarrel. African conversation can also be very

---

[27] Kwesi Yankah, *Speaking for the Chief: Okyeame and the Politics of Akan Royal Oratory* (Bloomington: Indiana University Press, 1995), 51.

slow and subdued, with significant pauses. This is the case, for example, when people are talking about serious matters, such as illness or death. Africans often punctuate their conversation with noises, such as mmm or mhmm, which are not words. It is usually appropriate, during conversation, to make various kinds of physical contact, such as shaking or clapping of hands. In certain situations, silence is as important as the words spoken, sometimes more important. Pausing and thinking about what has been said already, and what to say next, can be very important, especially in the conversation of elders.

In Africa, as elsewhere, the nature of conversation depends on the context and the status of the people involved, but there tends to be more formality in Africa than in America. Yankah notes, for example, that "in formal situations, a Ghanaian chief or king does not speak directly to an audience in his presence; he speaks only through his okyeame, who relays or repeats his words to the audience present, whose words to the chief must also pass through the okyeame."[28] In African culture generally, younger people do not normally speak in front of elders. If the occasion allows, they have to speak with the greatest respect. I tell my American students that I follow this custom faithfully; the notion of freedom of speech, so important to Americans, is not only irrelevant in such situations but also inappropriate.

In Africa, a person's freedom of speech increases with age. The oldest people have the greatest freedom, backed by real authority. What they say is the law in the community. Americans ask whether this applies to women as well. Age is so

---

[28] Yankah, 8.

important in Africa that the respect that comes with it cuts across the gender divide. One day, in the course of my folklore research with my team, we visited a Sukuma village in northwestern Tanzania. The old men of the village were sitting by themselves. Later an old woman appeared and walked to where they were sitting and sat down with them. Her age gave her the right to be with the old men. It was an interesting episode to behold.

Kitereza sums up some of these issues very well, when he explains why he wrote his book:

> ... I wanted this to be a way of preserving the language of our ancestors, by showing the reader how beautifully they spoke to each other, whether it was in their neighborly conversations during palavers in each other's homes or simply in the casual exchange of greetings between even total strangers who chanced to meet on the roads, who too would always politely exchange with each other greetings and news of wherever they were coming from and inform each other of where they were going.[29]

This is the African way of life, especially in the villages. As you walk along the path, you greet the people you meet, even if they are strangers. It is normal to have conversation and ask all kinds of questions, such as where the person is going. After you part, each person will meet other people and carry on conversation, in which they will certainly include what they have said or heard in the previous conversations. As a result, everyone knows about everyone else's affairs. A brother-in-law of mine

---

[29] Kitereza, ix.

38

once joked that in our culture, it is impossible to tell a lie. If you tell someone you are going somewhere, the news will spread, and people from where you said you were going will easily be able to confirm whether you went there on not, in their conversations with the other people.

Eye Contact

Whenever I hear or think about eye contact, I recall my early days in Madison. I used to note that, during conversations, the women looked right into my eyes. That intrigued me, but it also made me feel special. Here I was, in the center of America, being such an attraction to all the women. Only later, much later, did I learn that eye contact is a natural part of American conversation, and that what I experienced in Madison did not mean that I was a star, after all. That was a cultural experience I will never forget. In most cultures, eye contact between men and women has sexual connotations. Men, however, can maintain eye contact with other men, and women can do the same with other women without any problem.

In African cultures, avoiding eye contact is, usually, a sign of respect. It is not proper for children and young people to look into the eyes of old people during conversation. In *Mr. Myombekere*, Kitereza illustrates this well, and in his comments on the book, Ruhumbika notes, "A mother-in-law and her son-in-law were not allowed by Kikerewe custom to be near each other or to have their eyes meet."[30] In many situations, I instinctively avoid eye contact. I explain this to my American students, so that they know I am being respectful, just as someone from another culture might bow to show respect. Unfortunately, it would be awkward to explain this to every American I meet. One day, however, I got a real shock. I picked up a book by Deborah Tannen and stumbled across a section that said that people who don't make eye contact

---

[30] Ruhumbika, "Notes," 13.

are considered deceitful and unreliable. I was horrified to imagine that, all the years I had been trying to be respectful, I may have appeared to the Americans as unreliable or deceitful. On another day, some years later, my little daughter came home from school, and happily told me what she had learned that day: one of these lessons was the importance of eye contact. I know this is good education for life in America, but I am anxious about how she is going to cope in Tanzania.

One day, an American student came into my office to ask about her grade, which she was not pleased with. As we discussed her paper, she had her eyes fixed on my face. From my cultural perspective, nothing could be more impudent than this: a mere youngster coming to me with a complaint and staring at me like that. I was seething with anger, but I did my best to appear normal. We argued for more than half an hour, and, from all I could tell, because I was not gazing at her, she was staring at me all that time. I knew that Americans maintain eye contact during conversation, but that knowledge did nothing to diminish my fury. It was a dramatic instance of conflict of cultures. Fortunately, for her and me, I did not grab a cane and chase her out of my office, as a typical African would have done.

Let me end with some verses from a famous Sufi poet, Ibn 'Arabi, who lived 1165-1240 in Andalusia:

I had just kissed the black Stone
When some attractive **women**
   came hurrying toward me.
They had come to perform
   the ritual rounds,
Covering their faces with the veil.

41

They uncovered themselves,
They who were like the **rays of suns**.
"Restrain yourself!" they told me,
For the soul can be lost in eye contacts.[31]

[31] Ibn 'Arabi, *Perfect Harmony*, translation © Shambhala
Publications, Inc., calligraphy by Hassan Massoudy (Boston:
Shambhala, 2002), n.p.

Personal Space and Other Matters

I had never thought about the issue of personal space until the day I heard an American consultant addressing students who were going to study abroad. She asked them to think about the distance they maintain between themselves and the person they are talking to. Explaining that this varied from culture to culture, she said that Americans tend to stay about three feet away.

I thought about what Africans do, and I realized that they do not seem to care much for personal space in this sense. During conversation, they tend to involve much body contact, from patting each other to shaking and slapping each other's hands. Across Africa, there are different kinds of handshake used during conversation. Among Tanzanians, when people break into laughter, they spontaneously slap each other's palms, making a sharp loud clap. Whenever I provide orientation to American students going to Tanzania, I teach them how to perform this gesture. It is a very important gesture, like the American high-five.

In other ways, however, Africans do value personal space. Women occupy and operate in their own space, and so do the men. The segregation has more to do with respect than any other consideration. Outsiders might think it stems from, and reflects, discrimination and oppression. It would be disrespectful for a man to enter the women's space, and vice versa, except in special situations. When a husband and a wife are walking together, they maintain some distance between them, a respectful distance. In some cultures the man walks in front; in other cultures, he walks behind.

Africans don't feel at ease being alone, with empty spaces around them; they gravitate towards other people. As children in Africa, we used to read in European books that a man's best friend is his dog. That may be true for westerners, but for us Africans, our best friends are fellow human beings. I tell my American students that Africans do not go out alone exploring the woods and the flowers, as Americans might. If you see an African in the woods, he or she is probably looking for firewood, medicine, or a lost goat. Otherwise, people will consider such a person crazy.

Africans also dread silence, especially if it is prolonged; they want to hear human voices. Compared to the USA, Africa is a noisy place. Africans call each other across a crowd of people or across the whole village. Someone at the back of a bus might carry on a conversation with someone sitting far ahead. Drivers honk even when there is no apparent reason for doing so. Bars and nightclubs play loud music, for the whole world to hear. In the streets, in the market, and other places, there is loud music. Nobody complains. As Barley notes, "Africans seem genuinely perplexed by the Westerner's predilection for creeping around in silence when presumably he could afford enough batteries to have his radio playing day and night."[32] Africans do not see loud music as disturbance, except if it not good music. If the music is good, everyone wants it loud. I often hear African-Americans talking very loud, by American standards, and calling each other from afar. I enjoy that very much, and feel a special connection with them during those moments.

---

[32] Barley, 25.

Americans avoid encroaching on other people's time, privacy, and space. That is their way of respecting other people. Africans will see them as aloof, self-centered, and anti-social. Africans run into one another's lives all the time; they expect and thrive on such encroachments, viewing them as normal and acceptable behaviour. They go to each other's homes without appointments, and attend their neighbour's party without invitation. In fact, staying away from a neighbour's party is not only impolite but also unfriendly. The Africans don't complain about a loud party in the neighbourhood because they are all at the party; they are supposed to be. In any case, they don't see such noise as disturbance. In African cities, a wedding party will go through the streets, with people singing at the top of their voices, cars honking and trumpets blaring, and the people living on those streets will simply come out to enjoy the procession.

When Americans call me on the phone, they always ask, after I pick up the phone, whether that is a good time to call, whether I have time to talk. Africans never ask those questions. Once you pick up the phone, you are in deep trouble: prepare for a marathon conversation. The Africans take it for granted that you have plenty of time to talk. I tell Americans going to Africa that once they arrive there, they should forget their notions of personal time, space, and privacy. They should forget the notion of needing time to be by themselves.

Every culture has its notion of private matters and privacy. Private property is so central in the lives of Americans that it is virtually sacred. There are "no trespassing" signs everywhere, and Americans take them seriously. They will avoid parking on someone's property, for example. Africans have a somewhat different attitude. They can walk across someone's field, and, if it is not planted with crops, graze their cows and goats in it. They will even walk across someone's lawn to get to the house. Americans regard information about their age as a private matter. It is not quite appropriate to ask them how old they are. Many will not reveal their age even in their resume. Africans, on the other hand, freely ask such questions and feel good if they discover they are older than everyone else. Being old, older than someone else, or the oldest in a group, carries status and commands respect. Americans, however, desire to be young, or at least look young, for years and years.

One of the most daunting privacy challenges I faced during my early days in Madison is the way the American public bathrooms are built. They do not fully conceal the person inside. At least the shoes will be visible from under the door. I found this to be a great challenge, and still do, coming from a culture where such a facility is built in such a way that it completely conceals the person using it.

The Home

One day, an American colleague and I were driving down U.S. highway 35 from Minnesota to Iowa. I saw a mobile home being transported down the highway and was both fascinated and amused by the spectacle. I asked my colleague whether that thing speeding down the highway was a house or a home. We had a good laugh over this matter.

What is a home? Is a house necessarily a home? People from different cultures may occupy identical houses, but they do whatever they can to turn them into homes according to their cultural traditions and tastes. They will bring in carpets, art works, utensils and other paraphernalia. They will bring their customs, such as taking shoes off upon entering the house and leaving them at the door. Immigrants coming to America are no exception. After obtaining housing, they embark on turning those houses into homes. In doing so, they sometimes end up violating American laws. There are, for example, reports of immigrants facing legal troubles for slaughtering livestock on their premises, the way they would do in their home countries. While the authorities cite violations of city ordinances and other rules, the American neighbours recoil at what they see as cruelty to animals.

The African home is a complex institution, governed by many rules and charged with meanings. While approaching it, you call or announce your presence. In most parts of East Africa, one calls out the Swahili word "hodi." The host replies "karibu," meaning welcome. You repeat this formula at least once as you approach the door. It is important to study the proper procedure for every African society. Once inside the house, you stay in a certain area; the rest of the house is out of bounds. In my Matengo culture, a grown up would not go into his or her parents' bedroom. I do not go into my mother's bedroom, whether she is around or not. I would only enter it in case of an emergency, such as a fire. I was amazed, during my early years in the USA, at how readily Americans took me on tours of their homes, showing me all the rooms, including all the bedrooms. It was very difficult for me to look into the adults' bedrooms, and impossible to enter them. When the husband and wife opened their bedroom for me, I used to stand outside, unable to move, frozen with culture shock.

During the American war against Iraq in 2003, I saw a photo of an American soldier who had come into an Iraqi home to search for weapons. Members of the Iraqi family were sitting in chairs and couches, while the soldier stood there in the middle in military outfit, including boots. I told some Americans that I worried about that photo, and about the consequences of what the soldier was doing. It is improper to go into people's homes with one's shoes on, let alone military boots. I was sure that what that soldier was doing was a grave violation of the sacredness of that Iraqi home. Though the Iraqis in the photo looked calm, I could sense the rage in the hearts.

Later, I read that the Americans were introducing what they called a more culturally sensitive style of searching the Iraqi homes, prompted by Iraqi complaints about the soldiers searching women's rooms. The Americans were going to ensure that the women were out of their rooms before searching them. I felt this new approach was not culturally sensitive enough; it missed the point that there are areas in a home that outsiders do not enter, whether the occupants are there or not. I thought about my own culture; I do not enter my mother's bedroom, even when she is away. I heard a story about an American coming to an African village to do research. His host received him well, and later suggested they go out to see the village. The American had expensive equipment and other valuables, and he worried about their safety while he was out of the house, which did not have secure doors. The old man took the valuables to his own bedroom. It was no more secure than the other rooms, but who would dare violate the taboo about entering the parents' bedroom? Unfortunately, the young generation of Africans is slowly losing respect for these taboos.

One interesting thing in American etiquette concerns using the bathroom. When you are in an American home and need to use the bathroom, you ask: "May I use the bathroom?" The host will cheerfully show it to you. In Africa, people simply ask where the bathroom is, without the suggestion of seeking permission. In the villages, the toilet will be a clearly visible little structure away from the main house. All you have to do is excuse yourself, as you rise up, by saying the appropriate local euphemism for going to the toilet. In East Africa there are many such euphemisms. You can say, for example, that you are going to dig for medicine, the Swahili phrase being "kuchimba dawa."

Many Americans get to live with African families. This is challenging, for both the Americans and the Africans. Americans experience a mode of living that is different from theirs. First there are the basic things, such as the physical structures. Except in towns, cities, and some isolated cases in the rural areas, African homes do not have internal plumbing. Most Africans, particularly rural ones, would be appalled to have a bathroom in the house. African life revolves around the family, which embraces a couple, their children, in-laws, uncles, nephews, aunties, and many other people. As a result, the African home tends to always have people. People just come and go, without any prior notice. Relatives and guests come and stay as long as they wish. We do not ask people how long they are going to stay. Doing so is improper; it means, actually, one does not welcome the guest. It is up to the guest to say when he or she will be leaving.

Americans desire big houses, even if they have no children or people to live with. Africans will find this hard to understand. I recall the policy for allocating housing for faculty and staff at the University of Dar es Salaam, when I used to teach there. While the rent for everyone was the same percentage of their salary, those with families got bigger houses than those without; the allocation was based on need, not the amount of money one actually paid. We all felt the policy was just, because we acknowledge the importance of a family. Many Americans do not want children and are comfortable living by themselves, while children are a prime desire of the Africans--the more the better. I often read advertisements in American papers for house or apartment rentals, which include the condition that children are not allowed. Any African would find such rejections of children harrowing. Okot p"Bitek's *Song of Lawino* dwells on this issue, as Lawino complains about Ocol, her husband, who has adopted European ways and values. She says:

If a child cries
Or has a cough
Ocol storms like a buffalo,

He throws things
At the child;
He says
He does not want
To hear noises,
That children's cries
And coughs disturb him!

Is this not the talk
Of a witch?
What music is sweeter
Than the cries of children?

A homestead in which
The cries of children
Are not heard,
Where the short little songs
Are not repeated endlessly,
Where the brief sobs
And brotherly accusations
And false denials
Are not heard![33]

She goes on to ask what the value of a home is where children's excreta is not scattered around the swept compounds; where there are no children to break the pots and gourds.[34]

Africans are born and raised in homes usually teeming with people: family members, relatives, guests, children, youths and adults. Growing up in such circumstances, they learn on a daily basis various social skills as well as such basic things as sharing food and sleeping space. The

---

[33] Okot p'Bitek, *Song of Lawino & Song of Ocol* (Oxford: Heinemann Educational Books, 1988), 67.
[34] Okot p'Bitek, 68.

mere presence of so many other people around them makes this necessary. The adults are there to watch the children, guide them, admonish and punish them when they stray from the accepted norms. Every adult has this responsibility over any child, not just their own. An American child grows up shielded from some of these experiences. She expects and gets her own room in the home, where she plays her own games or watches television. This is possible because the home does not have as many occupants as an African home. In America, the idea of an adult, especially a stranger, sharing a bed with a child raises eyebrows. An increasing number of Africans, especially city dwellers and those who think they are educated, are imitating the western habits, such as keeping their children indoors, in front of the television sets, or playing indoor games. I wonder what the consequences will be in the future lives of these children. I have sometimes read about how these habits are affecting Americans, such as the case of newly-weds having to adjust to the challenge of sharing the same space.

I remember driving with my family around the beautiful Minnesota countryside in the summer, during our first year in this state. We would see homes, but no people at any of those homes. We found this strange and quite funny. In Africa, there are likely to be people around a homestead, on such warm and sunny days. There would be children playing outside some of the homes.

Many Americans keep pets, such as dogs, cats, birds, and fish and lavish much care and tenderness on them. They let their dogs wander anywhere in their house, even taking them in the car as they drive. They rush home from work or other engagement to walk their dog or feed their cat.

Americans will hug and even kiss their dog or hold their cat like a baby. When the Americans list the members of their family, they might include the dog, the cat or other pet. They are probably joking, but it would be insulting to list an African's dog as part of his or her family. I cannot imagine an African allowing a dog in his car, hugging it, or kissing it. Many Africans are Muslims, for whom dogs are unclean animals, just like pigs. While Americans buy special food for their pets, Africans generally leave their pets to fend for themselves: the dogs go about the village scavenging for bones, while the cats hunt for mice. The African dogs are not really pets but house guards or hunting animals. If a dog wanders into the kitchen or living room, the Africans chase it out with curses and a big stick.

Our Bodies

Our bodies carry cultural meanings, based on such aspects as shape, size, and complexion. They are like texts, which we read and interpret. Africans equate a fat body with prosperity and general happiness. They consider fat women beautiful, as we can see in the opening statements of "The Fat Woman Who Melted Away," an Efik-Ibibio folktale:

> There was once a very fat woman who was made of oil. She was very beautiful and many young men applied to her parents for permission to marry her and offered a dowry; but the mother always refused. She said it was impossible for her daughter to work on a farm as she would melt in the sun. At last a stranger from a far-distant country fell in love with the fat woman, and he promised, if her mother would give her to him, that he would keep her in the shade. At last the mother agreed, and he took his wife away.[36]

In the past, many African societies used to keep young women indoors, fattening them with special foods, in preparation for marriage. If you are thin, Africans think there is something wrong with you. If you are a married man, they might blame your wife for not taking good care of you.

Americans don't want to gain weight and be fat. It is not appropriate to call an American fat. I have heard stories of American women in Africa being upset when Africans called them fat. They

---

[35] Paul Radin, "The Fat Woman Who Melted Away," *African Folktales*, Paul Radin, ed. (New York: Schocken Books, 1983), 260.

54

didn't know that African men admire fat women and that many compliment women publicly, even if they don't know them. Americans struggle to lose weight, encouraged, if not pressured, by countless experts, or people claiming to be experts, as well as endless advertisements for drugs and therapies for losing weight.

Even though Africans value and admire the fat body, they do not discriminate against those who are not fat. Fat Americans, on the other hand, suffer unhappiness, alienation and even discrimination. Many suffer from what is called low self-esteem, a concept that Africans will find rather strange. There is more acceptance of body diversity in Africa than in America.

Americans also desire to remain young, or at least look young, despite the onset of old age. They seek various remedies against aging and remove the symptoms of aging, such as grey hair and wrinkles. Africans, on the contrary, value old age, since it brings respect and authority.

Concepts such as beauty and privacy are intimately connected with the body. In America, many people use the body to assert the concept of individual rights. Those who support abortion claim that this issue concerns the woman's body, and that only she has the right to decide whether to have a baby or an abortion. Africans do not think this way, because they do not isolate the individual from the family and the community.

For various reasons, people around the world do things to change the appearance of the body. Some Americans undergo plastic surgery or breast implants. The Maasai of Kenya and Tanzania pierce and extend their ears, while the Kalenjin of Kenya remove a lower tooth. Many of us fail to understand and respect the practices of other cultures, tending to regard them as odd or distasteful. Hemingway, however, had an interesting attitude: observing such practices in East Africa, he wrote that, when he got used to them, he realized that

> there was nothing odd or unseemly in the stretching of the ears, in the tribal scars, or in a man carrying a spear. The tribal marks and the tattooed places seemed natural and handsome adornments and I regretted not having any of my own. My own scars were all informal, some irregular and sprawling, others simply puffy welts. I had one on my forehead that people still commented on, asking if I had bumped my head; but Droop had handsome ones beside his cheekbones and others, symmetrical and decorative, on his chest and belly. I was thinking that I had one good one, a sort of embossed Christmas tree, on the bottom of my right foot that only served to wear out socks, when we jumped two reedbuck[36]

We use our bodies as a medium of communication. Whether we stand or sit in particular ways, make gestures, hold or shake our heads, make faces, or keep a certain distance between others and ourselves we are sending messages. Dancing is a form of language using the body. The messages we communicate with our bodies are different in different cultures. I was in India in 1991, and noted the way many Indians shake their heads to express agreement. They shake it in the way other people, including Africans, do when they say no. I had a hard time determining

---

[36] Hemingway, *Green Hills of Africa*, 52-3.

when the Indians meant yes and when they meant no. Pointing a finger at someone may be a normal or harmless gesture in some cultures, but it could be an offense in other cultures. Gestures are among the trickiest aspects of communication across cultures.

The American media helps shape attitudes concerning the body, including concepts of beauty. Advertisements use women's bodies a great deal, projecting a particular concept of a beautiful body. Race and skin colour also play a great role in defining the American concept of beauty. I had read about the psychological effects of racism, but America was the first country I visited where people pay so much attention to a person's appearance. I was amazed that even African-Americans differentiate among themselves according to whether one has light skin or dark. Some members of my own family in Tanzania are very light skinned, and others are darker, but it has never occurred to us to pay much attention to these differences.

African folktales and folklore dwell on the topic of the body in various ways. Many folktales depict characters who are handsome or ugly, characters with a physical handicap, characters who are half human and half beast, and characters who can change their shapes. In presenting the characters who are beautiful, the tales often seek to explore questions such as pride and arrogance, and in presenting characters who are handicapped, the tales tend to explore and stress the necessity for compassion towards all beings. They do this through rewarding or punishing the other characters according to how they treat these disadvantaged individuals. The "Tale of Two Women," in *Matengo*

Folktales, contains this theme.[37] The West African epic of Sundiata treats this theme in a moving way.[38]

In almost all cultures, people cover some parts of their bodies. However, there are wide variations across cultures on which parts are covered and how. We could say that we all cover at least the private parts, but the very notion of private parts is not uniform across the various cultures. In some cultures women cover their whole bodies, including their faces. In other words, there is no part of those women's bodies which is not private. There are some cultures, including a few in Africa, in which women go around bare breasted. American women may wear miniskirts, but they cover their breasts. It appears that breasts are truly private in American culture: American women won't even breastfeed their babies in public. African women, on the other hand, will pull out their breasts and feed their babies in public. It is normal for African women attending a class or a public meeting to be breast-feeding their infants at the same time. Africans don't even pay attention to this, let alone think about it. This is not surprising, given the love of children that permeates African life. The Africans acknowledge, without any reservation, the child's right to suckle her mother's breast. Nowadays, however, some African women under "western" influence hide their breasts while suckling. I think this is unfortunate.

While Americans desire choice and variety in clothing, the Maasai of Kenya and Tanzania use the same clothing style and a very limited set of colours, especially blue and red. They are happy that way,

---

[37] Mbele, 81-100.
[38] D. T. Niane, *Sundiata, An Epic of Old Mali*, trans. G.D. Pickett (London: Longman African Classics: 1995).

even though they see many different kinds of clothing in the shops. They are not, for example, interested in western clothing. Many Africans are Muslims. They tend to have distinctive attire. The women cover most of their bodies; many cover their entire face as well, leaving only the eyes. Some cover even the eyes. The African respect for old age requires that the older people get the more they cover themselves. This, however, is more so for women than men. It is inconceivable for an old African woman to wear shorts; even a skirt doesn't seem right for her. She may wear a dress or a skirt, but she will then wrap herself in a cloth that goes down to the legs. African children have much leeway; they can go about with the barest of clothing. Little girls, however, have to be more covered than little boys.

American culture seems to have fewer rules than African culture regarding clothing. Americans tend to dress casually, even in situations Africans might consider formal. I always see Americans going to church in quite informal attire. On American college campuses, students and many faculty and staff dress casually. Students even show up in class wearing torn jeans, t-shirts and caps. Africans go to the mosque or church dressed in a formal way. African students, from the first grade to the high school level, wear uniforms. College students dress well. When attending a funeral in Tanzania, or on the East African coast, women wear a khanga. In giving orientation to American students going to Africa, I explain all this and advise them take along appropriate formal clothing.

In the mid-nineties, I had American participants in my folklore research project in Tanzania. Among them were old ladies who sometimes wore shorts. It was quite an experience, moving around in remote Tanzanian villages with old American ladies in shorts. I knew that the Tanzanians were curious, if not amused, even though they kept quiet. The Americans, on the other hand, never seemed to realize they were quite a spectacle.

In rural areas, Africans keep their good clothes and shoes for special occasions, such as visiting relatives or going to Church or the Mosque. On ordinary days, they wear their work clothes, which, because of the nature of the work they do, are often shabby or tattered. The children, as well, do not wear shoes and good clothing as they play around the village or in the wilderness. When I am in my village, hoe in hand, weeding the coffee farm, I do not wear shoes or my good clothes. Western and other foreign media routinely present Africans in their unattractive or tattered work clothes, perpetuating the image of Africans as dirt poor. I showed American children a photo of children from my village, wearing nice clothes and shoes. The American children were not prepared for this. One of them, barely ten years old, could not contain his disbelief and confusion. He challenged me: "But Africans don't wear shoes!" I doubt if it would be better for the African children to sit at home the whole day, well dressed and watching television, than being out on the open plains and hills, playing as they do now.

Gender Issues

In African cultures, men and women operate in separate spaces. In the homes, there are sections for women and others for men. Men eat separately from the women. In my home area, in southern Tanzania, the gender segregation exists in the churches also. Men sit on one side and women on the other side. The Christian missionaries, from Germany, were wise enough to acknowledge and respect this aspect of the African culture. The Muslims, also, observe strict separation of men and women in the mosques.

All over Africa, there is gender-based division of labour as well; the men do certain kinds of work and women do women's work. Men are not supposed to do women's work, and vice versa. It is necessary, therefore, for a man to have a wife and for a woman to have a husband, since they complement each other. An unmarried person faces the unpleasant prospect of having to do work that is not his or hers. *Myombekere* depicts very well the plight of a man without a wife, the misery and humiliation he endures as he goes about doing women's work.

American students staying with African families find it difficult to cope with the gender segregation in African culture. They see women do all the work in the home, while men sit around and talk. The women serve the men. American men are not comfortable in this position, nor are American women, serving the men all the time. However, because they live in the African homes, they have to follow those customs. Driven by feminist ideals, some have even attempted to challenge these customs. I sympathize with the Americans, having spent enough time in their country to understand their perspective and feelings.

On the surface, African women appear weak and powerless, burdened and crushed by male domination. The reality is somewhat different. Deep in their hearts, the Africans know this. There is a proverb in Gikuyu, which states the point well: "Giathi githaragio ni gaka kamwe," A gathering can be dispersed by one small woman.[39] Wole Soyinka's play *Death and the King's Horseman*, set in Nigeria, offers a powerful demonstration of the strength of women.[40] Sembene Ousmane does the same in his novel, *God's Bits of Wood*, set in Senegal and Mali.

Relations between men and women can be tricky; they can be perilous, when the people involved are from different cultures. The most innocent word or move can send the wrong message and generate an unexpected reaction. What is appropriate in one culture may not be in another. It may even be offensive. Over the years, Americans have sharpened their awareness of the issue of sexual harassment. Colleges and other institutions have policies on the issue, with elaborate definitions of sexual harassment, including details of the various forms of such harassment. They publish literature and notices with relevant information, advice and warning, such as "No means no!"

I know, however, those rules don't work in Africa. I tell the American women that, in Africa, they will face countless propositions, from all kinds

---

[39] See Catherine Ndungo, "Social Construction of Gender with Special Reference to Gikuyu and Swahili Proverbs," *Fabula*, 43, 1-2 (2002), 65.
[40] Wole Soyinka, *Death and the King's Horseman* (New York: Hill and Wang, 1999).

of men--young, adult, and old alike—and that saying no won't stop them. These men's patience is legendary, though their persistence bothers some of the American women. The problem is that, in Africa, statements such as yes or no can always be negotiated, and African women may say no in order to see how sincere the man is. If she really means what she says, she may eventually use rude language. At that point, a man who is not serious enough will give up; the serious one will suffer the verbal abuse and keep trying. With this kind of background, of course, African men are likely to get into trouble in America. African cultures still follow what outsiders might call a double standard. While men can express their feelings towards a woman, women are much more restrained and are expected to be. Most men, however, tend to be polite, anxious to please the woman, since they do not want to ruin their prospects or bring shame upon themselves.

Africans take if for granted that everyone, upon attaining the appropriate age, has to get married and have children. African folktales deal again and again with this theme. In these tales, when a boy becomes a young man, he automatically goes looking for a wife, or asks his father to do so for him. In the same way, when a young woman reaches the appropriate age, young men come to woo her. Sometimes the parents will make the decision to look for a wife for their son, or a husband for their daughter. In *Matengo Folktales*, the opening statements of all the tales dealing with humans incorporate these themes. One tale begins: "There was a man with five children."[41] Another one begins: "There were once two women. Each of them

---

[41] Mbele, 55.

gave birth to a baby."[42] Another one begins: "There was a man, and he bore two children."[43] Yet another one begins: "There was a man. He had no child. He just lived liked that—childless."[44] A Maasai folktale, "The Woman and the Children of the Sycamore Tree," makes the same point in its beginning statements: "There was once a woman who had no husband, and she lived for many days in trouble. One day she said to herself, 'Why do I always feel so troubled? It is because I have neither children nor husband. I shall go to the medicine-man and get some children.'"[45]

Once married, the African couple has to produce a child as soon as possible. If they don't, everyone wonders why, and relatives start seeking solutions to the problem. Americans have different values. It is very common for married people to stay without children. Many say they need to postpone parenthood for various reasons, such as establishing themselves economically. One can understand these sentiments, because Americans tend to focus on the nuclear family: the husband is the principal and perhaps only companion of the wife, and vice versa, and the children have only their parents to depend on. Africans not only want children right after marriage, but they also have an extended family and the broader community to help take care of the children. If a couple has difficulty taking care of a child, that child can go live with an uncle, and a distant cousin can pay school fees for the child.

Seeing an American man or woman who is single, the Africans assume that he or she has not

---

[42] Mbele, 81.
[43] Mbele, 101.
[44] Mbele, 114.
[45] Radin, 179.

found a suitable spouse and is still looking. During one of my research trips in Tanzania, with a number of westerners, we visited a Sukuma old man. He called me aside, at one point, and asked me to tell the young American woman in my group that he had a son who was looking for a wife, and she looked like the ideal woman. How many cows will her father want as dowry? I conveyed the message to the young woman. She took the question in style and replied that, unfortunately, the airplanes would not carry cattle to America. The old man thought about this for a moment and agreed.

As is the case around the world, Africans imagine America as a land of opportunity. They believe that marrying an American is a sure way to get to this fabled land. When they see an American, therefore, they get to work in earnest. Some American women become exasperated, if not offended, by the endless stream of men who propose to them, and, in particular, by their persistence. Although most of the men have good intentions, cultural differences, including the different ways of communicating, play a role in aggravating such situations. From my experiences in Madison, I suspect that the American habit of maintaining eye contact contributes to the misunderstandings. When American women look the African men in the eyes, they raise the men's hopes. Saying no while maintaining eye contact, they send mixed signals, both intriguing and enticing. Asking whether the Americans can learn to talk without maintaining eye contact would be like asking me whether I can learn to maintain eye contact. I don't think it will be easy, and maybe it will not be possible.

Africans don't know that many Americans prefer to remain single; nor do they know that being single in America does not carry the kind of stigma that it does in Africa. Even if they knew, they would not understand why anyone would want to remain single. It would be pointless to even try to tell the Africans about issues like sexual preference, as Americans understand them. The only thing that Africans know and care about is that everybody needs to get married and raise a family. I remember reading an article in *Ebony*, the famous African-American magazine, about what it called a successful African-American woman: she was well educated, with a good job, and single. This was, obviously, an American concept of success. In Africa, the fact of being single would have been a major drawback on that woman's profile. An African woman would count children as a principal measure of her success. In Okot p'Bitek's *Song of Lawino*, Lawino makes the point well:

> At the lineage shrine
> The prayers are for childbirth!
> At the *ogodo* dance
> The woman who struts
> And dances proudly,
> That is the mother of many,
> That is the fortunate one;
> And she dances
> And looks at her own shadow.[46]

Africans visiting the USA can be misled by what appears to be an open attitude to sex. The word sexy appears constantly in everyday American English, whether oral or written. The media and television shows are filled with sexual scenes, themes or references. There are adult bookstores in

---

[46] Okot p'Bitek, 68.

many places, which sell books, magazines, tapes, and other materials with explicit sexual content. Colleges offer classes and workshops on sexuality. Faced with all this, Africans might conclude that Americans are sexually very open and available. The media images, in fact, drive Africans to have illusions about the American women they encounter in Africa. Being in America, however, the Africans will, sooner or later, discover, and perhaps be puzzled, that many Americans are not as sexually active as the media might suggest, and many are not interested in the opposite sex. Whether they are in Africa or in America, Africans take it for granted that every person is heterosexual. The African cultures, through methods such as initiation practices, ensured that this was the case. I have not seen evidence in African folklore traditions or in the writings of the early travelers in Africa, or anthropologists, to suggest otherwise.

African men and women who respect themselves, or want to be respected, don't show affection in public: hugging, kissing, or holding hands. Nowadays, however, there are young men and women in African cities who form relationships with Americans or Europeans and don't mind breaking this rule. Having seen movies, read books and magazines or even traveled abroad, they know that Americans and Europeans hug, embrace, or kiss in public. In Africa, men can walk around holding hands, and women can do the same. In the dance halls, men can dance with fellow men, and women can dance with other women. None of these things mean that the people involved are gay or lesbian, as would sometimes be the impression in America.

There is a great deal of joking between African men and women, which is culturally appropriate and mutually entertaining, even though much of it involves sexual references. There is a difference between sexual banter and sexual harassment. Wole Soyinka's *Death and the King's Horseman* brims with such banter. The joking between men and women in Africa is part of a longstanding tradition, which involves not only individuals but also whole clans and ethnic groups. In Mali, for example, the Keita clan has a joking relationship with the Toure clan. Africans might not know that what is mere sexual banter in Africa is not acceptable to the Americans. Problems can arise when African men apply these cultural practices to American women.

Money Talks

Money talks, the saying goes. Is this true in all cultures? Does money mean the same thing in different cultures? In America, money is so central that many cultural values revolve around it. Even the language Americans use reflects this. The saying that money talks is instructive, as is the saying that time is money. For Americans, money is the measure of many aspects of life; they define poverty and riches, for example, in terms of money or the things that money can buy. When Americans hear about a place in the world where people live on less than two dollars a day, they think that means the people are desperately poor. If we were to ask the people themselves how they define poverty, or whether they see themselves as poor, we might discover some surprises. Poverty and wealth are cultural concepts. Among certain people in Africa, cattle are the measure of wealth, and also the measure of a man's intelligence. In meetings, only those who have cattle have the right to speak, for they have demonstrated their intelligence by obtaining and owning cattle. If you don't have cattle, you have nothing to tell the people, and, therefore, you have no right to address them. In Achebe's *Things Fall Apart*, a man's wealth consists of wives, children, titles and barns full of yams.

Americans take money very seriously. They keep track of it, wanting to know where every cent comes from and where it goes. They are alert to any opportunity to make money. Listen to these American proverbs: "A dollar saved is a dollar made;" "Lend a dollar, lose a friend;" "Your best friend is your dollar." "A quick nickel is better than a slow dollar;" "Save a dollar and keep your worries away."[47] One pays for virtually everything in America. I look at the luggage carts in American airports; they are secured is such a way that you cannot take any without depositing money. In the airport in Dar es Salaam, the carts are just lying around; you pick one and put your luggage in it, free of charge. The Tanzanians don't even realize that they could make money with those carts.

When Africans get money, they think about spending it: sharing it with relatives, for example, or throwing a party. There is a character in *Things Fall Apart*, Unoka, who does this all the time. The Matengo have a drinking song, which makes the point perfectly. The person with money starts and leads the song, as he buys drinks for fellow revelers, who all sing together:

Ng'ombila nee;
ng'ombila nee, nguli mali gaa;
ng'ombila nee;
ng'ombila nee, nguli mali gaa.

Applaud me;
applaud me, as I consume my wealth;
applaud me;
applaud me, as I consume my wealth.

The age-old tradition of the harvest festival is alive and well in Africa. Though all societies had it in the past, and many still maintain it, the Americans seem to have largely lost it.

The famous Swahili poem, *Utenzi wa Mkunumbi*, set on the Kenya coast, describes a competition in the town of Mkunumbi, in which the

---

[47] Judith Reitman, *American Proverbs*, (New York: Hippocrene Books, Inc. 2000), 43.

competing groups try to outdo each other in slaughtering cows for massive feasts.[48] The white district commissioner intervenes, to stop what he considers wastefulness. For the Africans, such spending boosts the reputation of a person or a group and their respect in the community. Just watch Africans at a musical performance. When they get excited, they spring up and dance all the way to the stage, where they mingle with the performers, showering money on their favourite performers. Others throw money on the stage to express their appreciation. The person who gives away the most money gains the greatest admiration and respect of the audience and the performers. The generosity of patrons, in turn, inspires the artists to do even better.

Africans look for money not for its own sake, but to build, maintain and strengthen social relationships and networks. That is their insurance policy and investment portfolio. If an African starts a shop in the village, people will come not only to buy goods but also to talk, pass the time, and borrow things. If a close relative comes to buy goods, the shopkeeper has to figure out whether to take the money, or how much. If the mother-in-law or the father-in-law comes, the equation changes completely. Only a fool or a crook would take money from a mother-in-law or a father-in-law and have peace of mind afterwards. As a result of all this, an African's shop might not make a profit, let alone expand. It may not be a successful business, in western terms, but it is an important and vital institution in the African village, because of its social role, and that is its success.

---

[48] Lyndon Harries, ed. *Utendi wa Mkunumbi* (Dar es Salaam: East African Literature Bureau, 1967).

Americans value money so much because they need to save for old age and also pay their many bills. In America, when people stop working, they need to be self-sufficient; they do not count on being supported by their children, as is the custom in Africa. Often, one sees very old Americans still doing hard jobs for wages, instead of resting as African elders do. America is a land of bills; people worry and talk about bills all the time. America appears wonderful, warm and friendly, but that is only as long as you are paying your bills promptly. If you do that, you get friendly letters from banks, credit card companies, car dealerships and marketing companies telling you what a wonderful person you are, and offering you deals and incentives to buy more. When you go shopping, they receive you with smiling faces. After you pay for your purchases, they thank you and, with a broad smile, tell you to have a wonderful day.

Arriving in America, Africans will surely be enchanted and mesmerized by the smiles in the commercials and the hospitality in the stores. They are used to the African markets and shops, where there is real friendship, and the vendors don't turn sour, or turn you away, because you don't have enough money, but will haggle with you over the price, and will even let you go with the goods, on the promise of finishing the payment later. Africans might think that the American businesses operate the same way.

Before I understood the American business world, I used to enjoy the friendliness. Nowadays, generally, I am neither touched by the smiling faces, nor happy when they wish me a nice day. I know only too well that, the day you run out of money, they are not going to be friendly, and they are not going to wish you a nice day. If you owe the

American banks, credit card companies and other institutions and cannot pay according to their schedule, they will turn hostile and inflict on you one trouble after another: finance charges, late fees, and harassing phone calls. If these measures fail to make you pay, you will deal with menacing threats from shadowy groups called collectors, of whom you knew absolutely nothing.

The work of the collectors is to terrorize debtors, making their life miserable, until they pay what they owe. Collectors have the authority to come and seize whatever property they can from the debtor--from cars to furniture--and auction it in efforts to recover the debt. This is the plight of millions of Americans. The banks, credit card companies, car dealerships, the collectors and other institutions of that kind have overwhelming power, to which Americans submit totally, the way other people submit to the will of God. In America, people can ignore and even defy God, claiming it is their right, but no one dares to defy the financial institutions. Defying them brings drastic and painful consequences. Africans need to know all this, in order to understand why Americans take money so seriously.

Africans tend to be casual about debts. They may not pay debts on time, and they are flexible with debtors who don't pay on time. In any case, there are no real deadlines in Africa; everyone knows that somehow the debt will be paid, even if little by little. With appropriate excuses, smooth diplomacy, and offers of a little beer from time to time, or a live chicken, debtors maintain friendly relations with the creditors. In Achebe's *Things Fall Apart*, Unoka hardly pays his many debts. Even though everyone laughs at him for being lazy, he continues to be a popular entertainer. People sometimes swear never to lend him money again, but in the end they do. He never becomes the hated enemy of any of his creditors. Although it would be both untrue and unfair to say that Unoka represents all Africans, Achebe offers a deep insight into an aspect of African culture that all Africans can relate to. I read an article in a Tanzanian newspaper, about a great sum of money the Zanzibar Government owed the Tanzanian Electric Supply Company (TANESCO). Noting that TANESCO was waiving the 15 billion shillings interest on the debt, the article reported:

> This was revealed yesterday by the Deputy Minister for Water, Works Energy and Land, Mansour Yusuf Himid, when answering a question in the House of Representatives. Mwembemakumbi Representative, Machano Othman Said, had wanted to know why the Zanzibar government had not been able to pay the 33.4 billion debt to TANESCO. Himid said the electricity bills had accumulated to the staggering sum because the government had no culture of settling bills on time.[49]

Coming to America with these attitudes, Africans easily land in deep trouble. I did not know, for example, that in America, there are things called credit reports, which indicate a person's record with creditors. If you don't pay debts on time, your credit record could suffer. Americans do whatever they can to build and maintain a good credit rating. For years, after landing in America, I just lived as if I were in Africa. I did not bother to scrutinize every bill I got and pay it on time. I thought that it did not

---

[49] PST correspondent, *The Guardian*, June 15, 2004.

matter whether I paid on time or late. I paid fines for late payments, but I thought that was all there was to it. Little did I know that I was digging my own grave, for I later discovered, to my dismay, that my credit rating was terrible. It was not that I did not have the money; I was simply not used to monitoring and paying all bills, including the smallest ones, on time. I did not know that there are secret organizations in America called credit-reporting agencies, which keep track of you. I had read George Orwell's famous phrase, Big Brother is watching you, and in America I learned how this works.

Americans express the connection between money and credit in a memorable proverb: "No man's credit is as good as his money."[50] In America, a bad credit report is some kind of stigma. If you have a bad credit rating, banks call you a bad risk; they won't lend you money, except with very stiff conditions, and you will respect the genius of Shakespeare, in the way he created Shylock, that implacable moneylender.[51] Only when such bad things happen does the African wake up, but it is too late. Whenever I visit Africa, I look around and see differences between American and African life. Once, in a little village in the Tanga region of Tanzania, I observed a small group of men sitting idly on the veranda of a house, arguing endlessly on different topics. They seemed to have no care in the world, and I started thinking how lucky they were, compared to people who live in America. These villagers did not have to worry about credit card debts, loan payments, car payments or credit reports. Though they seemed very poor by

---

[50] Reitman, 40.

[51] Shakespeare, *The Merchant of Venice.*

American standards, they did not have the pale, haggard, and exhausted looks I see on the faces of many Americans, who slave almost round the clock to try and keep up with their bills.

It appears that Americans truly believe in self-reliance and self-sufficiency. They would rather suffer in silence than go to a neighbour to borrow money, the way Africans do. Africans don't hesitate to borrow, whether money or a little salt for cooking the evening meal. I have learned much in my dealings with Americans. I know, for example, that when Americans invite you to dinner at a restaurant, it is wise to take your own money along. Africans assume that the person who invites you will pay. In America, usually, when the bill comes, it is split according to what everyone ate or drank. In the beginning, this ritual of splitting the bill was a real culture shock to me. I am still not used to it, but find it somewhat depressing.

Since their attitudes towards money are so different, when their dealings involve money, Americans and Africans should either be very patient with each other, or brace themselves for trouble. The Americans might view the Africans as undisciplined or even corrupt in their spending habits, and the Africans are likely to view the Americans as tight-fisted and mean. Whenever I got money from American institutions for assignments in Africa, I always ended up in some trouble upon my return. I could not account for all the money I had spent. Americans expect receipts for all expenses, while the culture of counting every coin and issuing receipts is not common in Africa. Where do I get a receipt for a trip I may have taken through the African countryside, riding as a passenger on someone's rusty motor-cycle or perched on the top of a truck loaded with people, firewood and dried fish? To cut a long story short, I always ended up paying from my own salary the money for which I did not have receipts.

Gifts

Americans often wonder what gifts they can give to their African hosts or friends. This is an important and also tricky question. It depends on the nature of the gift and the kind of person to receive the gift. Money is a suitable gift, so are gadgets like cameras and watches. Sometimes, people will ask for something specific, such as the pair of jeans you are wearing; those are easy situations. Apart from such clear-cut cases, there are many shady areas. It is best to ask someone in the culture about what is an appropriate gift in each situation. Clothes make good gifts, but one has to be careful about giving used clothes. I noted, during my first years in the USA, that Americans don't hesitate to give others used clothes. When our baby was born, people brought clothes, some of which their own children had used as babies. When our baby had outgrown those clothes, those people asked for them, for their own or other people's babies. Africans are still somewhat jittery about all this, even though used clothes are quickly becoming a fact of life.

In many parts of East Africa, the khanga cloth is a most suitable gift for women. On special occasions, such as Christmas and the Muslim holiday of Idd el Fitr, a man will make sure to buy a pair of khanga for a woman he loves or cares for. This custom is so ingrained that people offer khanga to American and European women as gifts on such occasions as bidding them farewell. At the appropriate moment during the ceremony, the Africans will normally wrap the khanga around the foreign women, with much clapping of hands and shrill ululations from the audience. It is a great honour to be so treated. Khanga is not a gift for men, the only exception being that a woman might give a piece of her khanga to her lover.

There are gifts suitable for African children, such as toys, pens and pencils, as well as gadgets like simple watches, cameras and small amounts of money. If one is not sure whether a certain gift will be suitable for a family or not, it is safest to offer it to children, in front of their parents. If you call a child, talk to her and give her five dollars, for example, or even more, in front of her father or mother, everybody will appreciate it. It is also proper to avoid giving someone a gift in the presence of outsiders. If you are in doubt about how to give a gift to someone, it is best to use an intermediary, who can do so in the appropriate manner. In the course of my folklore research in northwestern Tanzania, I once went with my team to interview a chief. After the interview, as we were preparing to leave, I, of course, wanted to offer the chief a token of gratitude. I called one of my associates aside. He was from that area and knew the local language. I gave the gift to him, a certain sum of money. A little while later, as the conversation was still going on, since saying goodbye is an elaborate process in such situations, he privately called an official of the chief aside and gave him the gift. We left the village knowing that the official would do the rest.

One problem Americans face in Africa is that Africans ask them for money and other things all the time. The Americans feel overwhelmed and, generally, come back feeling frustrated, because they were not able to grant all the requests. I tell them a number of things. People around the world believe Americans are rich; this makes them make those requests. In African cultures, the wealthy person in the family, clan, or village shares his or her wealth with the ones who have less wealth. The Africans view the Americans in the same light. In the same way, they consider any African who works for Americans as being well off and expect this person to share the wealth with relatives, friends, and neighbours. The more generous this person is, the more respect and admiration he or she gains in the community. The American gains the same respect and admiration by being generous.

Sometimes Africans ask for money and other things only to get a conversation going, or as a form of joking, to see how well you can take a joke, and therefore how sociable you are. When someone asks for something you don't have or don't want to give away, you can treat the request as an invitation to a conversation. You can respond with a good-natured joke: say that you need a chicken and would really be happy to exchange money for a chicken, instead of worrying for not having what the person is asking for. Other people, of course, may be asking in earnest. In any case, they ask for things they might not have, and would be quite happy to give you, in return, something they do have, such as a chicken, some eggs, a bag of flour, or a bunch of bananas. Feel free, as part of the conversation, to ask for such things. Exchanging gifts is part of African culture. It creates a bond, and, some day, the person you give a gift to could prove valuable; he or she could grant you help, such as introducing you to an important official. In traditional African society, it was appropriate to approach the chief and offer him some gift, such as beer or livestock. Such offerings paved the way for asking a favour from the chief later. Nowadays, we do not look deeply into the intricacies of these social practices; we jump on the bandwagon and denounce everything as corruption.

Africans like to offer gifts to guests. In the rural areas, these gifts tend to be things the villagers themselves produce: a bunch of bananas, a few eggs, beans, or a live chicken. In my Matengo culture, the gift of a live chicken is a great honour. The guest departs carrying the chicken under the arm, and can go into the village bus with it.

One interesting custom I observed in the USA concerns the opening of gifts. During a ceremony in which gifts are given, the recipient will open the gifts in front of everyone, and that is expected. Africans don't open the gifts, until everyone has departed. I used to find it challenging, in the USA, to have to open gifts in public. I would be standing there, holding the gift, with the excited Americans exclaiming: "Open it!"

Time Flies, but not in Africa

Do Africans and Americans view time the same way? I don't think so. I was once in the post office in Arusha, Tanzania, during my research trips to Tanzania. There were many of us standing in line, waiting to be served. The line was taking a long time, and one young white woman, who had become impatient, said to an African man next to her, "In Africa, there is always waiting!" The man nodded in agreement. I found myself thinking about this, wondering whether there is anything wrong with a culture in which there is so much waiting, and nothing seems to happen on time, as Americans would say.

Americans want things done promptly and according to a fixed schedule. They wake up knowing, or wanting to know, the day's schedule. They want action, and value being busy all the time. Africans take their time and follow what is called African time. To Americans, Africans seem never on time; meetings in Africa never seem to start or end on time. The buses never seem to arrive or depart on time. The Africans have watches and clocks, but they do not allow these gadgets to control their lives. In Africa, Americans have to learn to wait for things to be done or to happen. Why are Africans never on time, so to speak? It is because they have a different concept of time, and a different understanding of what is really important in life. An African may leave his house early, intending to be on time for an appointment. On the way, he may meet friends or relatives. He cannot ignore them, simply because of an appointment. In Matengo culture, if you encounter a funeral procession on the way, you must help carry the casket, no matter where you were going.

When Africans set out on a journey, they do not necessarily think in terms of going straight to their destination and arriving on time. For them a journey could be an opportunity to do many things on the way, such as visiting people who happen to live along the way. Whenever my father and I went to some nearby or distant villages, we would always stop to greet people we met, or we would deviate from our way and visit people. My father's eyes would wander away from the path, scanning the bushes around. He would go into the bush to pick up some medicinal herb, or to check a tree branch that might be suitable for making handles for hoes or some other implements. Digression is integral to African life; it happens not only in journeys, but also in other activities, such as meetings, conversations, and storytelling. Such activities rarely have a fixed timeframe or trajectory: they are flexible and open-ended.

When I was growing up, in rural southern Tanzania, people would say to my parents: "We will visit you on Saturday." They never specified the time of day, and no one asked them to. All that mattered to us was that guests were coming on Saturday. We would be on the look out for them, whether we were at home or away in the fields. When an African says he or she is coming in five minutes or ten minutes, don't take it literally. Such a statement merely expresses a wish or a desire to come as soon as possible. The Africans understand that other things could intervene: one could meet friends or acquaintances on the way, for example. One cannot rush past them without greeting them or talking with them. Greetings often take much time, depending on the person one encounters.

Delays and waiting do not bother Africans the way they bother Americans. If someone fails to show up on time, Africans might not even notice it, because they might be busy exchanging greetings, talking, or doing other things anyway, unless the person is really late. Otherwise, they just assume that something must have happened, and they carry on with other tasks. If the bus is late, which is usually the case, the Africans simply wait or go and get busy with other activities, until the bus comes. When Africans are late for an appointment, they might not apologize, or they might talk about it just casually. They do not mean to be disrespectful, only that from their cultural standpoint, being late is not really an offence, except on certain occasions.

Is the American way better than the African way? Should the Africans learn to be punctual? It sounds only sensible to say yes, but I am afraid there are ethnocentric biases in these demands and expectations. Punctuality is much valued in certain cultures, such as the American one, but it is not a universal value. All cultures have their own priorities, and sound reasons for doing things their way. A culture may look disorganized to outsiders, but it has its own mode of organization, its own logic. A culture does not have to change simply to accommodate or live up to some external standards and expectations. Yet this is the desire and agenda of what are called development agencies and development programs. They seek to force Africans into western molds. I know that the world is getting more and more interconnected and that cultures are under pressure to abide by certain rhythms, but apart from essential adjustments, cultures should be free to be themselves, without being pushed around or denigrated.

Americans think that time flies; they see it in terms of units of hours and minutes, each of which must be used, filled with activity, and accounted for. For Africans, time is always there; if they cannot finish something today, there is always tomorrow. As I have said, when Americans phone me, they will always ask whether I have time to talk, or whether it is an appropriate time to call. Africans never ask such questions. The moment you pick up the phone, they just launch into a lengthy conversation, taking it for granted that you have all the time in the world to talk.

Americans open and close offices, business premises, and other institutions according to a strict schedule. I remember my early experiences with the bars in Madison. Just before closing time, the bar tender would shout, "Last call!" That was to invite people to buy their last drink. When the minute for closing came, the same bar tender would vigorously order people out. It was amazing to witness the dramatic change from hospitality to aggression. I never got used to this experience.

In Africa, things tend to be different. At the closing time, the owner of the bar might close the door, but people who had bought drinks before that time would continue drinking inside. The owner might merely close the counter where the drinks are sold, while continuing to sneak in to get more drinks for the customers. As long as the doors are closed, the police do not normally care what might be going on inside the bar. In the USA, on the other hand, when the door was closed, it meant there was absolutely no one still drinking inside. Banks follow the same pattern. In America, if a bank closes at 12:00, it is closed. You cannot go and knock on the door after that time. In Africa, even if the bank is closed, and you come some minutes afterwards, you can knock on the door and start pleading, saying, for example, that you need the money for food for your children. The bank staff will surely listen to your pleas, though they might respond with complaints or harsh words. But if you persist and present a truly eloquent and moving tale, they will certainly serve you, unless the person who must sign the necessary paperwork is gone. In Africa, the bank is truly closed when the bank workers are gone. The fact that the doors are closed does not mean that the bank is necessarily closed. In America, people follow the written rules. If they arrive half a minute after the doors close, they just go back, and will not even think of bothering the bank workers or the postal workers as Africans do.

Truth and Lies

Truth and lies may seem like simple matters to figure out and differentiate. We encounter surprises, however, as we look at different cultures. In Africa, for example, things can be complicated, as Hemingway noted:

> In Africa a thing is true at first light and a lie by noon and you have no more respect for it than for the lovely, perfect weed-fringed lake you see across the sun-baked salt plain. You have walked across that plain in the morning and you know that no such lake is there. But now it is there absolutely true, beautiful and believable.[52]

What Hemingway says about the African landscape applies to the African culture. There is much flexibility and even ambiguity in what people say. Africans can say no even when they mean yes, and vice versa. They leave open the possibility of further conversation, in which matters can be negotiated and clarified. If they feel that saying no might hurt or disappoint the other person, they are likely to give a vague answer or even say a non-emphatic yes. I heard a story about a white man traveling through African villages in the olden days. He knew the name of the place he was going, but he did not know how far it was. As he walked and walked, he would come to a village and ask if where he was going was far or not. The villagers would say it was not far. He kept walking, and stopping at

---

[52] Ernest Hemingway, *True at First Light*, ed. Patrick Hemingway (New York: Simon &Schuster, 1999). 189.

every village to ask; everywhere they told him it was not far. The white man kept going, not happy at all, and realizing that the Africans cannot be trusted. Now were the Africans telling lies? Why didn't they say that the place was far or very far? For the Africans, the situation determines whether to tell the truth or not. In this case, the important point for the Africans was to avoid discouraging the traveler. It was important to keep his spirits high. Telling the stranger that the place was not far was a way of helping him, not lying. Africans will say a place is only two miles away, when, in fact, it might be three, four, or more miles. For them, distance is not necessarily a matter of miles; it can be a mere mental construct, to suit the occasion.

Africans find it difficult to refuse requests directly; asked to do something they don't want to do, they might say: "I will try," or they might agree or seem to agree and then not do it. They can promise to come and then not come. They aim to please rather than displease. The failure to come creates a kind of vagueness in the air; the person waiting might not know why the other person did not come. This lack of certainty is a cushion against the blunt impact of an outright refusal. It creates room for conversation later, including the giving of explanations and excuses.

Africans also think about saving face. When they have done something wrong or embarrassing, they might not admit it directly. Even witnesses might focus more on saving the wrongdoer from undue embarrassment than on exposing or confronting him or her, especially if the person has status in the community, such as an elder. Writing about the Giriama of Kenya, Ronald Ngala states:

Wagiriama, kama makabila mengine, wana desturi nyingi za adabu, ambazo zote zakaza heshima hata mara nyingine mtu huona ni adabu kusema uongo ili aonekane na heshima machoni pa wengine.

The Giriama, like other ethnic groups, have many customs which signify good breeding, and all of which emphasize respect to the extent that sometimes a person feels it is congruent with good breeding to tell a lie in order to be seen as respectful before the eyes of others.[53]

To let the truth out and also save face, Africans might make evasive, vague, or ambiguous statements, coming to the point only as a last resort.

Americans speak directly; they say what is in their mind, whether yes or no. They expect direct answers to questions. If they disagree with you, or if you have done something wrong, they will tell you directly, whether you are young or old. If they have bad news they will say it. A common American statement goes: "I have some good news and some bad news." Having said that, they will go ahead and state both the good news and the bad news. Even in the hospital, American doctors tell the patients their condition, while an African doctor will do whatever is necessary to avoid discouraging the patient. If it becomes really necessary to break bad news, the African doctor will do so to a close relative of the patient, the representative of the patient's

---

[53] Ronald G. Ngala, "The Wagiriama," in *Swahili Readings*, ed. Alfons Loogman, C.S. Sp, (Pittsburgh: Duquesne University Press, 1967), 55. My translation.

family. The family members will also leave the patient in the dark, to the end.

Work and the Work Place

Americans take work very seriously. They will cut short a conversation in order to be at work on time. While there, they focus on working. Africans don't kill themselves trying to be at work on time. If they are in America, they have to, of course, but let us just talk about Africa. When the Africans arrive at work, their first priority is greeting and talking with other workers. They must find out how everyone is doing, and how their families are. They need to catch up with the latest news and gossip. Only after this ritual is done do they drift somehow into the routine of working. Even then, they take the workplace as a place not just for work but also for socializing. They like talking with other workers, while working, or instead of working. It is fine to visit Africans at work, sit down and carry on a conversation. Unless they urgently need to finish something, they will welcome you, feeling honoured that you visited them. Afterwards they will escort you and continue the conversation outside. Africans do not record, the way Americans do, the amount of time they spend working. The African workplace is usually slow and easy-going.

Americans work very hard and expect everyone to do the same. They work so hard that many suffer from work-related stress. I doubt if Africans know what this is, except if they live in the USA. Africans who are in the USA bitterly complain about the backbreaking work they have to endure. Americans do not normally visit others at work nor do they expect the kinds of random visits that are part of the African work place. When you need to visit an American at work, you set an appointment. You can be sure that he or she will be there, working hard and waiting for you. You can make appointments with Africans, of course, but be prepared for anything.

Africa is steadily changing, as American and other multinational enterprises move in. This creates challenges, including the emergence of workplaces with a culturally diverse workforce. As they work together, can the Americans, Africans and other people identify their cultural differences and find the best ways to manage them? How, for example, do they handle the issue of punctuality? Can the American investor, for example, make the Africans conform to a strict sense of time, and how does he or she deal with workers who come late to work? What if they state reasons for being late, such as I have mentioned? Should the American pay attention to those reasons or should he or she dismiss them? What about gender issues? Should the workplace post rules about this, the way it is done in the USA? If so, whose rules should these be, the African ones or the American ones? Should such a work place accommodate or incorporate the local culture? All these are key questions. I think that the more an enterprise accommodates the local culture, the more motivated and happy the workforce will be. The opposite will result in dissatisfaction, resentment and alienation.

There is, also, the issue of the relationship between employers and employees. When you employ Africans, you should pay attention to Barley's words:

> A man who works for you is not just an employee: you are his patron. It is an open-ended relationship. If his wife is ill, that is as much your problem as his and you will be expected to do all in your power to heal her.

92

If you decide to throw anything away, he must be given first refusal on it. To give it to someone else would be most improper. It is almost impossible to draw a line between what is your concern and what is his private life. The unwary European will get caught up in the vast range of loose kinship obligations, unless he is very lucky indeed. When an employee calls you 'father,' this is a danger sign. There is surely a story about an unpaid dowry or dead cattle to follow and it will be perceived as a genuine betrayal not to assume part of the burden.[54]

Barley views the matter with an outsider's detachment, but makes quite accurate observations. The Africans do view the employer like a parent, or like the chief, who has to help his people in times of need and to be generous in that regard. When an African employee is in financial need, he might of course approach friends for help, but he can also approach the employer for such help, especially a salary advance. Employers and employees consider this normal. After coming to the USA, I realized that Americans go to the bank for loans of all kinds, whether small or large, personal or for business. Back in Africa, I always thought that one needed a bank loan only for major projects such as establishing a business or building a house.

I wish to share one more story. My home computer was having problems. I told an American technician about it. He said he would be happy to come, and that he charged fifty dollars an hour. The idea of paying by the hour dampened my spirit. On previous occasions, I had called a guy from El

---

[54] Barley, 40.

Salvador, a recent immigrant to the USA. I would go and get him, since he did not drive. While he was working on the computer, we would be talking and joking about everything under the sun. We would offer him some beer to sip as he worked. When evening came, we would eat dinner together. By nighttime, however, the   job was done. He would take another beer. On at least one occasion, he fell asleep on the couch. When it was time to go, I would drive him back. On the way, I would ask him what I owed him. He would say something like twenty dollars or thirty. It did not matter how many hours he spent at our house: he just figured out the whole experience and stated the fee. I liked this guy; he came into our house not just as a computer technician but also as our guest.

Conclusion

In many ways, African culture resembles the African market. Crowded and noisy the African market displays the vitality and exuberance of African life. The language of the market place is vibrant and full of humour, as haggling develops into spirited joking. A bond develops between buyer, seller, and spectators, which is precious in ways the exchanging of goods for money is not. Like many other contexts and situations in Africa, the market is a place for building relationships.

Though the African market seems like a scene of great confusion, it has its own rules. When you go into the market, you see many vendors, each hoping you will be their customer. You will end up buying from one, two or three of them, of course, depending on what you need. Just remember that this is not just a commercial transaction but also a social one. It is a good idea to have conversation throughout the buying process, about yourself and your family, your travels and occupation, about the vendor, his business, family, and other things. Time spent this way is not wasted.

On the first day, you may not be able or comfortable enough to haggle over the price. A little haggling, even just as a friendly joke, means a great deal to the African vendor. The only problem is that if you are a foreigner, especially a white person, people think you are rich, and it is thus not good to haggle too much. The next time you go into that market, and on all subsequent occasions, look for the same vendor. Everyone who may have seen you the first time will know that you are this vendor's customer. If you ignore this vendor, you are violating some unwritten rule. You will benefit by developing the bond with your original vendor. You will get a decent price, because of the developing friendship. You might get some goods for free. Your friend might even invite you home to meet his family. It is all about relationships.

I cannot claim to have mentioned all the possible issues and challenges Americans and Africans might encounter when they interact. Nor can I claim to have done justice to the issues I have raised. My understanding of America is based largely on my experience in the mid-western states of Wisconsin and Minnesota. My friends in those states always reminded me that the mid-west is not the USA. When I told them that Africans are easy-going, they told me that Californians are that way too. One day, in a hotel in New York, I met an elderly California couple on their way to Uganda. When I told them about African time, they told me that Californians are always late, about fifteen minutes.

I started by recalling my days as a graduate student in Madison, during which we Africans used to talk and joke about American ways. Writing this booklet has made me realize that we were dealing with culture shock. Now I understand why many Americans in Africa stick with other Americans. Should I blame them if they also talk and joke about African ways? It is clear to me, now, that we all tend to do the same thing. To criticize them alone, and not my African network in Madison as well, would be to use a double standard.

I have learned that if Americans seem aloof, it is primarily because they value their privacy and the privacy of others. Once there is a reason or an opportunity, they will get close to you. I realized this when my wife had a car accident and was hospitalized for a week in Minneapolis, fifty miles away. My American colleagues, who had all along seemed busy and distant, closed ranks around my family, bringing food to my house for the whole week and making sure that my children were fine. I used to believe that we Africans are the most caring people in the world, but seeing how these Americans sacrificed themselves for the sake of my family gave me much food for thought. This is not an isolated case. Whenever Americans learn about a problem anywhere in the world, they want to do something about it. This mentality drives Americans into various situations around the world. It is unfortunate that people who criticize Americans for imperialistic tendencies often don't know this aspect of the American national character. Yes, there is American imperialism, but the American public as such is also driven by humanistic considerations.

We may talk about culture, in the sense of patterns of acting, beliefs and values, but in the final analysis, economic factors shape culture. American culture is what it is today largely because of the forces of capitalism which are also transforming African culture. Understanding the American financial system has helped me understand why Americans are so careful with money. One of the most important lessons I have learned in thinking about cultural differences is that, when people of another culture say or do things that I don't like or understand, I should consider that it could be due to cultural differences. For example, Americans appear to other people rude and abrupt, while, in fact, they might just be talking in their usual American way. Similarly, if Africans appear to often ignore or bend rules, it is not because they lack principles but because their lives revolve around the principle Jesus stated so well: the Sabbath was made for man, not man for the Sabbath.

I hope this book serves some useful purpose, even if only to stimulate discussion. I always welcome opportunities for such discussions, in any manner: email messages, one-on-one conversations, group meetings, seminars and workshops. Working together, we can make the world a better place for all of us and for future generations. To learn more about my work and my dreams, please visit my website: www.africonexion.com.

Bibliography

Achebe, Chinua. *Things Fall Apart.* London: Heinemann, 1981.

Afokpa, Kodjo Jb. "Greeting Performance in Eʋeland: Ethnographic Background and Cultural Analysis." *Southern Folklore*, 48, 3 (1991). 205-233.

Aidoo, Ama Ata. *Dilemma of a Ghost and Anowa.* London: Longman African Writers, 1995.

'Arabi, Ibn. *Perfect Harmony.* Trans. Shambhala Publications, Inc. Boston: Shambhala, 2002.

Barley, Nigel. *Adventures in a Mud Hut: An Innocent Anthropologist Abroad.* New York: The Vanguard Press, 1983.

Brown, Ina Corrine. *Understanding Other Cultures.* Englewood Cliffs: Prentice Hall, Inc. 1963.

Chilson, Peter. *Riding the Demon: On the Road in West Africa.* Athens: University of Georgia Press, 1999.

Fanon, Frantz. *The Wretched of the Earth.* Trans. Constance Farrington. New York: Grove Press, 1963.

----------. *Black Skin White Masks.* Trans. Lam Markmann. New York: Wiedenfeld, 1991.

Harries, Lyndon. *Utendi wa Mkunumbi.* Dar es Salaam: East African Literatue Bureau, 1967.

Hemingway, Ernest. *Green Hills of Africa.* New York: Simon and Schuster, 1996.

----------. *True at First Light.* Ed. Patrick Hemingway. New York: Simon & Schuster, 1999.

Kitereza, Aniceti. *Mr. Myombekere and his Wife Bugonoka, Their Son Ntulanalwo and Daughter Bulihwali.* Trans. Gabriel Ruhumbika. Dar es Salaam: Mkuki na Nyota Publishers, 2002.

Mbele, Joseph L. *Matengo Folktales*. Haverford: Infinity Publishing.com, 2001.

McElroy, Colleen. *Over the Lip of the World: Among the Storytellers of Madagascar*. Seattle: University of Washington Press, 1999.

Ndungo, Catherine. "Social Construction of Gender with Special Reference to Gikuyu and Swahili Proverbs." *Fabula*, 43, 1-2 (2002). 64-74.

Ngala, Ronald G. "The Wagiriama." In *Swahili Readings*. Ed. Alfons Loogman, C.S.Sp. Pittsburgh: Duquesne University Press, 1967. 53-62.

Niane, D.T. *Sundiata: An Epic of Old Mali*. Trans. G. D. Pickett. London: Longman African Classics, 1995.

Ousmane, Sembene. *God's Bits of Wood*. Trans. Francis Price. London: Heinemann, 1970.

P'Bitek, Okot. *Song of Lawino & Song of Ocol*. Oxford: Heinemann Educational Books, 1988.

PST Correspondent, "The Guardian." Dar es Salaam. June 15, 2004.

Radin, Paul. *African Folktales*. (New York: Schocken Books, 1983). 260-61.

Reitman, Judith. *American Proverbs*. New York: Hippocrene Books, Inc. 2000.

Richburg, Keith B. *Out of America: A Black Man Confronts Africa*. New York: Basic Books, 1997.

Ruhumbika, Gabriel. "Chapter 1: Notes." *Mr. Myombekere and his Wife Bugonoka, Their Son Ntulanalwo and Daughter Bulihwali*. Trans. Gabriel Ruhumbika. Dar es Salaam: Mkuki na Nyota Publishers, 2002. 12-15.

Shakespeare, William. *The Merchant of Venice*. Ed. W. Moelwyn Merchant. London: Penguin Books, 1987.

----------. *Julius Caesar.* Ed. David Bevington. Toronto: Bantam Classics, 1988.

Soyinka, Wole. *The Road.* London: Oxford University Press, 1965.

----------. *Death and the King's Horseman.* New York: Hill and Wang, 1999.

Yankah, Kwesi. *Speaking for the Chief: Okyeane and the Politics of Akan Royal Oratory.* Bloomington: Indiana University Press, 1995.